IS IT TRUE?

A NEW WINDMILL COLLECTION EXPLORING LITERARY NON-FICTION

EDITED BY ROS HICKS AND LINDA NEWBY

Heinemann Educational Publishers
Halley Court, Jordan Hill, Oxford OX2 8EJ
Part of Harcourt Education

Heinemann is the registered trademark of
Harcourt Education Limited

Selection, introduction and activities © Ros Hicks and Linda Newby, 2004

First published 2004

09 08 07 06 05 04
10 9 8 7 6 5 4 3 2 1

British Library Cataloguing in Publication Data is available
from the British Library on request.

ISBN 0 435 13098 6

Photographs: p21 Topham; pp44, 46, 56, 93, 95, 125 Corbis; p165 Getty News
and Sport; p171 PA Photos.
Cover design by Forepoint
Cover photo: © Escher/Cordon Art BV
Typeset by 🖎 Tek-Art, Croydon, Surrey

Printed and bound in the United Kingdom by Clays Ltd

Acknowledgements

Every effort has been made to contact copyright holders of material
reproduced in this book. Any omissions will be rectified in subsequent
printings if notice is given to the publishers.

Extract from *Toast: the story of a boy's hunger* by Nigel Slater, published by
Fourth Estate 2003. Copyright © Nigel Slater 2003. Reprinted with permission
of HarperCollins Publishers Ltd; extract from *Cider With Rosie* by Laurie Lee,
published by The Hogarth Press. Used by permission of The Random House
Group Ltd; extract from *Bad Blood* by Lorna Sage, published by Fourth
Estate. Copyright © Lorna Sage 2000. Reprinted with permission of
HarperCollins Publishers Ltd;

(continued on p214)

Contents

Introduction for students

'Is it true?'

People often ask this question about a piece of writing. Whether or not we are being told the truth makes a difference to the way we react to what we read.

What are the different kinds of non-fiction?

You probably know the differences between fiction, which is 'made up', and non-fiction, which is 'true'. Examples of non-fiction include letters of complaint, encyclopaedia entries and school reports. What is less clear is the difference between ordinary, everyday non-fiction and literary non-fiction.

What makes a piece of non-fiction literary?

When you write about real events, real people, or real places, you are dealing with facts or 'non-fiction'. The way you handle these facts and make choices about how you use them can make the reader see them through your eyes. For example, you may choose to highlight some things but not to mention others. Because you have been selective, the reader gets a *version* of the truth, not necessarily the whole truth.

Literary non-fiction is different from other non-fiction in the following ways:
- It explores ideas rather than just presenting the facts.
- The writing is crafted so that it will affect the feelings of the reader.
- It uses language in lively and imaginative ways.
- Attention has been paid to the sounds of words and rhythms of sentences.

- It may use the patterns and structures of fiction writing to create impact, for example, conveying feelings of tension or drama.
- It is written to last, to be appreciated as a piece of writing and not just to perform a short-lived job or function.

This collection

All the extracts in this book have been selected to help you enjoy and appreciate the richness of literary non-fiction. Each section includes extracts written in different circumstances, with writers responding in different ways to communicate a variety of feelings, emotions and ideas.

We hope that you will gain insights into how writers use their craft to communicate and that you, in turn, will explore and experiment with some of their techniques to create some literary non-fiction of your own.

Ros Hicks
Linda Newby

Introduction for teachers

Literary non-fiction has grown in profile in the National Curriculum for English, and has recently become a separate requirement for the first time. But how do we recognise and define it? How might the teaching of literary non-fiction be approached differently from the teaching of fiction? This collection is designed to tackle these questions, exemplify the genre and clarify its characteristics.

How do we recognise literary non-fiction?

Defining literary non-fiction is something of a minefield. In attaching the term 'literary' we must consider the writing style, which inevitably leads to the thorny issue of literary merit. Good writers of literary non-fiction have to make clear linguistic choices to convey a variety of ideas with freshness and clarity. Factual material is crafted; ideas are reflected on and elaborated. This is as true for literary science writing as it is for autobiography.

There are also ethical questions to be considered in selecting and teaching literary non-fiction. The material must be factual, but the writer must do more than simply present the facts. The facts are selected and manipulated to engage the reader. These processes can easily distort the truth, and this brings into question just how far a writer can stray from the truth whilst maintaining the trust of the reader. This is a complex area, but one that is worth exploring. The final section of the collection, Fact and fiction: exploring why a writer chooses to blur 'truth', encourages readers to make their own judgements about how writers select information to give particular perspectives.

In trying to distinguish literary non-fiction from more straightforward non-fiction, the analogy of a skeleton may be useful: the bare bones are the facts that provide the framework on which to build something more interesting and powerful. For example, in writing about the courage of his fellow soldiers in *Goodbye to All That* on pages 139–42, Robert Graves deploys a range of devices to convey bleakness and despair as well as showing his own taut anger about the situation. He lets the reader in on the experience. This is much more than a factual account of life in the trenches.

What are the characteristics of literary non-fiction?
We have signposted the hallmarks of literary non-fiction in a number of ways. First, we have provided a list of features that characterise literary non-fiction:

* It explores ideas rather than just presenting the facts.
* The writing is crafted so that it will affect the feelings of the reader.
* It uses language in lively and imaginative ways.
* Attention has been paid to the sounds of words and rhythms of sentences.
* It may use the patterns and structures of fiction writing to create impact, for example, conveying feelings of tension or drama.
* It is written to last, to be appreciated as a piece of writing and not just to perform a short-lived job or function.

Next, the introductions to each sections and each extract draw students' attention to the most interesting characteristics. These are then explored further as the focus of the accompanying activities.

Finallly, at the end of the collection, in *Routes through the collection*, we have mapped out the key features of each extract as well as its type and purpose. This makes it easy to cross-reference, group and select extracts for different approaches, ensuring that the collection is flexible to use.

How is this collection organised?

Literary non-fiction appears in many guises: letters, biography and travel writing to name but a few. Awareness of text type and purpose is important, but we felt it would give a better sense of the variety and richness of literary non-fiction if we did not constrain the organisation into those 'types'. So, for example, in the 'Historic events' section there are three extracts about the *Titanic*: an eyewitness account, an emotive newspaper report and a piece describing the discovery of the wreck. Grouping them together and drawing attention to the literary craft with which the writers convey the impact and significance of events, enables readers to understand the powerful characteristics of literary non-fiction expressed in a variety of forms.

Another reason for grouping texts in this way is the difficulty of defining them by genre. Was Pepys writing a diary, a memoir, or social commentary? How does travel writing overlap with autobiography? Much literary non-fiction is hybridised, so it is important not to oversimplify the text types. As students progress across Key Stage 3, they should encounter texts that do not fall into neat categories. This collection will help them develop skills of discrimination and judgement about purpose, style and audience that will help them succeed in the greater demands of GCSE.

How can you use this collection?

This book can be used in a variety of ways. The extracts are often grouped together because there are strong links between them. For example, each of the extracts in Section 1 presents and develops a view of a character, thus disclosing the particular relationship between that character and the writer. They also engage and connect as a group through their focus on food. When extracts have been juxtaposed in this way, it is indicated in the section introduction.

There are other ways of planning a journey through the collection. We have included a balance of extracts written before 1914, extracts from different cultures and traditions and material written by and about individual men and women. The extracts also have a range of purposes that can be grouped across different sections. So, for example, it would be possible to use the grid on pages 204–6 to identify a range of extracts that use humour to entertain, and to focus on how different writers achieve this.

How are the activities structured?

The activities are sequenced to support students' exploration and understanding of the extracts through a range of close reading tasks leading to linked writing tasks designed to develop the skills of reflection and independent response. In this way, a focus on word- and sentence-level objectives scaffolds writing. This scaffolding supports both critical writing and more creative, imitative responses. There are also activities designed to encourage students to compare extracts through themes, ideas and language.There are clear connections to the English Framework objectives and, like the Key Stage 3 Strategy, we aim to encourage students to read with a writer's eye and write with a reader's eye.

Finally ...

It is of the greatest importance that students experience a range of thought-provoking literary non-fiction texts that illuminate their own experiences and enable them to understand how writing is crafted to do this successfully. We hope that this is what this collection will do.

Ros Hicks
Linda Newby

Section 1

Viewpoints: seeing through a writer's eyes

This section looks at the work of writers who describe people and places in lively, funny or moving ways. While reading the extracts, it may be helpful to keep the following questions in mind.

- How do writers use humour to create affectionate pictures of people they know well?
- How do writers craft their language and structure to bring people and places alive for the reader?
- How do writers use language and structure to express their views about people and places?

Extracts in this section

Why the extracts have been selected

Extracts 1–3 all reveal the character of cooks in amusing ways, although the character in Extract 3 is less affectionately drawn than those in the other two.

Extract 4 is an enthusiastic description of a city and a particular event that happens there, through which the writer makes his viewpoint clear.

Extracts 5–7 are from different cultures. All three writers create a warm picture of the central character through the choice of the events they relate and the language and structure they choose.

Extract 8 is a vibrant picture of life in another country. The writer's feelings for the place are evident in the sounds, rhythms and images evoked through her choice of language.

Spaghetti Bolognese
by *Nigel Slater*

In this extract from his food-centred autobiography, the writer uses language and structure to recreate tension, humour and vivid characters. As you read this extract you should focus on:

- the use of dialogue to provide humour
- how the piece is structured to create humour
- the use of similes and metaphors
- the use of interesting adjectives and verbs.

The writer is now a famous cookery writer and spaghetti bolognese is regarded as quite ordinary food, but when he was a boy this dish was regarded as new and strange. This is his family's first attempt at cooking and eating this exotic dish.

'We ... are ... going to have ... spaghetti, no, SPAGHETTI ... just try a bit of it. You don't have to eat it if you DON'T LIKE it.' Mum is yelling into Auntie Fanny's 'good' ear. Quite why she thinks there is a good one and a bad one is a mystery. Everyone knows the old bat is deaf as a post in both.

Neither Fanny nor Mum has eaten spaghetti before, and come to think of it neither have I. Dad is waiting for the water to boil on the **Aga**. The sauce is already warm, having been poured from its tin a good half-hour ago and is sitting on the cool plate of the Aga, giving just the occasional blip-blop.

When the water finally boils my father shakes the strands of pasta out of the blue sugar paper that looks for

---

Aga heavy cooking stove

all the world like a great long firework, and stands them in the bubbling water. They splay out like one of those fibre-optic lights we saw at the Ideal Home Exhibition on the BBC. As the water comes back to the boil he tries to push the spikes under the water. 'They'll never all go in,' he snaps, trying to read the packet, which, even when read with bifocals, is in Italian. Some of the brittle sticks break in half and clatter over the hotplate.

'Will I like it, Daddy?' I ask, half hoping he'll change his mind and Mum will cook us all some chops.

'Just try it,' he says, a somewhat exasperated tone creeping in to his voice. 'Just try it.'

'I think you should put some salt in,' chirps in Mum.

Auntie Fanny is looking down at her lap. 'Do I have to have some?' I think she is going to cry.

'I think it must be done now,' says my father twenty minutes later. He drains the slithery lengths of spaghetti in a colander in the sink. Some are escaping through the holes and curling up in the sink like nests of worms. 'Quick, get the plates, they're getting away.'

We all sit there staring at our tumbling piles of pasta on our glass Pyrex plates. 'Oh, Kathleen, I don't think I can,' sobs Auntie Fanny, who then picks up a long sticky strand with her fingers and pops it into her mouth from which it hangs all the way down to her lap.

'No, wait for the sauce, Fanny,' Mother sighs, and then quite out of character, 'Come on, Daddy, hurry up,' Dad spoons the sauce, a slurry of reddy-brown mince that smells 'foreign', over the knots and twirls of pasta. Suddenly it all seems so grown-up, so sophisticated.

Mum wraps the strands around her fork, 'like this, do it like this,' then shovels it towards Fanny's wet, pink little lips. Most of the pasta falls down Fanny's skirt, a little of the sauce gets caught on her bottom lip. She licks it off and shudders. 'It's horrible, it's horrible. He's trying to poison me,' she wails. We all know she would have said the same even if it had been the most delectable thing she had ever eaten.

Ignoring Fanny's little tantrum, I do as Mother did, twirling the pasta around my fork while shovelling the escaping pieces back on with my spoon. I rather like it, the feel of the softly slippery noodles, the rich sauce which is hot, salty and tastes partly of tomato, partly of **Bovril**. I wouldn't mind eating this every day. Unexpectedly, my father takes out a cardboard drum of grated Parmesan cheese and passes it to me to open.

'What's that you've got there?' asks Mum.

'It's grated cheese. Percy Salt said you have to sprinkle it over the top. It doesn't work if you don't.' Now we're talking. I peel away the piece of paper that is covering the holes and shake the white powder over my sauce. I pass it to my father who does the same. Mum declines as she usually does with anything unusual. There is no point in asking Auntie Fanny, who is by now quietly wetting her pants.

Dad shakes the last of the cheese over his pasta and suddenly everyone goes quiet. I'm looking down but I can see my father out of the corner of my right eye; he has stopped, his fork in mid-air, a short strand of spaghetti hanging loose. His eyes have gone glassy and he puts his fork back down on his plate.

'Daddy, this cheese smells like sick,' I tell him.

'I know it does, son, don't eat it. I think it must be off.'

We never had spaghetti bolognese or Parmesan cheese again. Or for that matter, ever even talked about it.

Bovril beef extract

Cider with Rosie
by *Laurie Lee*

This humorous, affectionate description of a family situation gives insights into the character being described. As you read this extract you should focus on:
- the lively, imaginative use of language
- the attention that has been paid to the sounds of words and rhythms of sentences.

In this autobiographical book the writer tells of the many amusing and sometimes moving events of his childhood. The Lee children were brought up by their charming but rather chaotic mother. This extract describes the preparation of breakfast.

Walking downstairs there was a smell of floorboards, of rags, sour lemons, old spices. The smoky kitchen was in its morning muddle, from which breakfast would presently emerge. Mother stirred the porridge in a sootblack pot. Tony was carving bread with a ruler, the girls in their **mackintoshes** were laying the table, and the cats were eating the butter. I cleaned some boots and pumped up some fresh water; Jack went for a jug of skimmed milk.

'I'm all behind,' Mother said to the fire. 'This wretched coal's all slack.'

She snatched up an oil-can and threw it all on the fire. A belch of flame roared up the chimney. Mother gave a loud scream, as she always did, and went on stirring the porridge.

'If I had a proper stove,' she said. 'It's a trial getting you off each day.'

mackintoshes raincoats

Bad Blood
by *Lorna Sage*

This extract presents a domestic situation in a humorous way. As you read this extract you should focus on:
- the use of lively imaginative language
- the methods by which the writer creates humour.

The writer was a child in the 1950s, just after World War II. In her autobiography, she brings alive the troubles of her childhood and the strangeness of her family. Her recollections are both painful and funny. This extract is one of the more amusing parts of the book, although she reveals little affection for her mother in her humour.

You might have mistaken her for an aspiring vegetarian, but in fact the thought that we were eating the very lambs that went bleating to market in Dad's trucks didn't move her at all. She didn't care for farm animals. And if anything, she thought vegetables even more dangerous and difficult to subdue. They had to be cooked all morning, particularly green ones like sprouts, which got very salty and stuck to the pan as their water boiled away, and came out in a yellow mush. Potatoes got the same treatment and her ritual Sunday lunchtime cry, as she lifted the saucepan lid – 'They've gone to nothing!' – became a family joke, an immortal line that later converged magically in my mind with the smartest 1950s intellectual slogans. *Gone to nothing* was wonderfully Absurd, a phrase of **existentialist** and **sub-Beckettian**

---

existentialist to do with the idea of free will; suggesting that the potatoes had chosen to disappear

sub-Beckettian like a line from a play by Samuel Beckett, who was known for his theatre of the Absurd

power. As for my mother, she should be so lucky was her meaning – if only those wretched roots full of eyes *would* go to nothing! But no, there was a grey sludge left at the bottom of the pan (we never needed to mash our potatoes) which had after all to be spooned resignedly on to our plates.

Dinner on this scale only happened once a week, although, since it was a custom that survived into the 1960s, I can still recall my mother's recipe for lumpy gravy. You take the pan of fat in which the meat has been frazzled, add water from the vegetables (and since there's never enough left, top it up with cold from the tap), then add flour, and cook for quite a while, pursuing the lumps into the corners with a spoon and crushing them to make more. Then add Gravy Browning so that there's no mistaking them and serve with a sigh.

Luckily no one lives by Sunday dinners alone. The real revelation for the ending of **austerity**, for us, was ready-made food, the whole rich list of things that needed no cooking at all, which you could eat at any old time. For instance: ham and tongue cut into see-through slices; sandwiches of meat-paste or fish-paste or bananas; canned corned beef, luncheon meat (Spam in civilian clothes), pilchards, sardines, salmon, baked beans and spaghetti; tinned peaches, pears and plums, and fruit salad with mauve 'cherries', and condensed milk. These goodies – eked out with cornflakes, puffed wheat, digestive biscuits, cream crackers, crisps and sweets – would constitute our staple diet. We actually called them in leftover language 'the rations' and they were delivered once a week by the village grocer in his van.

In the matter of food, in fact, market forces were on my mother's side. Beefburgers and tinned rice pudding and processed cheese and even sliced bread itself were all just

---

austerity life without luxuries

the kinds of things she wished for, pills under various guises. I have a persistent but suspect memory that she was somehow involved in consumer-testing fish fingers and **infallibly** foresaw their future role as everyone's 'rations'. Surely **Hanmer** couldn't have figured in such a survey? I must be remembering the satisfaction with which she greeted their advent. Fish was to her possibly nature's most nightmare offering – covered in scales and fins, full of bones and very nourishing, so that you were obliged to struggle with it. In fish fingers nature was grandly snubbed and outdone. Their very name mocked the unreasonable design evolution had come up with for fish; and their bland and boneless insides left her nothing to worry about. They didn't need gravy, either.

So food got easier as time went by. Not all our meals aspired to the condition of fish fingers, but there wasn't a lot that could go wrong with (say) baked beans on toast. True, the beans were stewed (with extra water) to be on the safe side. And toast could be tricky (I was quite grown up before I learned that you didn't have to make toast by burning the bread and then scraping off the black bits) but on the whole, even if you allowed for sharp crusts and crumbs that could go down the wrong way, it did solve the problem of what to put in front of us.

---

infallibly without any possibility of being wrong
Hanmer the writer's home village

My Place – Wolverhampton
by *Philip Newby*

This essay gives a lively picture of a place by highlighting a particular event. The writer also expresses his point of view about the place in which he lives. As you read this essay you should focus upon:
- the use of language to express enthusiasm
- the use of vocabulary associated with young people
- how the structure conveys a point of view.

Students are often asked to write about the place in which they live. Here, a young writer takes an unconventional look at Wolverhampton.

Despite its unfashionable reputation for waning industry, soaring drugs problems and lack of class and culture, Wolverhampton is a really cool place in which to live.

If you lived in my street you could walk into the city centre or to a nature reserve, both within minutes; you could reach the very vibrant city of Birmingham, great for shopping and entertainment, by train, bus or Metro and get home again in the evening without a problem; you could count people of great cultural and racial diversity among your friends and neighbours and you could be sure that you lived in a place where young people are deemed important. We have a theatre, an art gallery, cinemas, concert halls, great sports facilities, a famous football club, a newly opened, council-owned, free skate park – and we have GENERATION.

I recall the second ever occasion on which this under-18s night club was opened. In the city and surrounding area, unusually for a Friday night in most places, play parks and Playstations were abandoned, *EastEnders* was left to the old folk and street corners were uninhabited by the drinkers of cheap, illicit cider.

Instead of taking part in the usual celebrations of the coming of the weekend, a large proportion of the city's youth were queueing outside the Wulfrun Hall, awaiting the opening of under-18s club night, 'Generation'. Even before seven, when the doors were set to open, there were large crowds of teenagers, talking in groups, most wearing t-shirts or hoodies, pledging their allegiance to a **plethora** of bands from Sum 41 to Tool. Amongst the throng the young people ranged from 10-year-olds wearing home-made Slipknot boiler suits to 16-year-olds with elaborately gel-crafted eight-inch spikes sticking out of their heads, trying to act as if they were above all that was going on around them.

Everybody passing through the doors was frisked by the larger-than-life security guards, determined that this should be a no-drugs, no-alcohol, no-real-trouble occasion. In fact, the whole building seemed to be awash with security, all seeming quite bemused by the spectacle of teenagers flinging themselves at each other in the middle of the Wulfrun's at-first-reluctant-to-fill dance floor. For many of the clubbers this was their first experience of a real mosh pit and they based their behaviour on the experiences related by older friends or siblings or on their excessive viewing of MTV2.

---

plethora a huge number

Their naivety would have ensured injury at any more adult event but here, for the time being, they were safe.

The DJ was intent upon feeding the crowd what they wanted, keeping up a constant stream of thrash metal, with every other record being Slipknot or Korn. The introduction of Blink 182's pop punk anthem 'The Rock Show' put a stop to the moshing, while Sum 41's 'Fat Lip' saw the crowd swarming back into the pit.

By the end of the evening everyone was on their feet, at least until their feet and legs disappeared from underneath them in the crush, or they were knocked down by other kids crowd surfing over the top of them, heedless of the warning of the security guards.

The first 'Generation' had been DJ'd by Radio One Rock Show presenter Mary Anne Hobbs, but even without the celebrity presence, the night was well attended. This monthly event is still very popular amongst young teenagers who dress up and chill out with their friends on a proper Friday night out. I know that many other towns and cities now have similar events for under-18s, but Wolverhampton's was the first of its kind and 'Generation' is just one of the reasons why I was glad to grow up in the heart of this often-berated city.

A recent *Panorama* programme may have labelled my home town the crack centre of the country and this is certainly a worry to parents, carers, teachers and youth workers, but, in truth, this problem has never impinged upon my life and I continue to be proud to be born and brought up in Wolverhampton.

Remembering Aunt Marie
by *Grace Nichols*

This autobiographical short story is interesting for its humour and for the way characters are revealed through events. As you read this piece you should focus upon:
- the use of lively, interesting language features to reveal character
- how dialogue reveals character
- how the writing reveals as much about the narrator as about her aunt
- how the writer structures the piece to make it amusing.

Grace Nichols was born and educated in Guyana but has lived in Britain since 1977. Remembering Aunt Marie *is a lively piece of writing about a larger-than-life family friend and about a particular incident that took place during a visit.*

Aunt Marie wasn't our real aunt but like all the big people who visited us had to be **prefaced** with Aunt, Uncle or Cousin. To call any grown-up 'full-mouth' – that was by their first name – was asking for trouble since it showed a lack of respect. As children we didn't mind in the least. The more aunties and uncles we had the merrier.

Like the trade winds that blew and the hot sun outside, Aunt Marie was a natural part of our lives. She had grown up with my mother and visited us nearly every day. You could always hear her voice floating ahead of her as soon as she entered our yard. 'O, God, Edna, a cup-of-tea, a cup-of-tea, the wind, the wind,' she would wail. She kept

---

prefaced she had to be called 'Aunt' as a sign of respect

up this tea-wailing all the way up our back steps, rubbing her stomach and depositing herself on the sofa with a modest belch.

This was the signal for my mother Edna to make her a cup of tea, and who could blame me for thinking that Aunt Marie's stomach was one great big knot of wind that could be **assuaged** only by endless cups of tea?

Another source of worry to Aunt Marie not unmixed with pride, were her bunions which protruded like two small onions just below the insides of her big toes. These had meteorological powers since they could predict the weather. Whenever it was going to rain, Aunt Marie's bunions would act up, leaving her **prostrate** on one of our beds, crying out from time to time: 'O God, the bunions, my name ain't Marie if it don't rain.'

More often than not she was proved right and so caught between the 'wind' and the 'bunions' as she was, Aunt Marie far outshone the other cousins and aunties who visited our home.

Aunt Marie had grown up in a convent, for she was only ten years old when her mother died, and her father, a Portuguese businessman, thought it was best. Since I always kept my ears cocked as a child to adult stories and 'big people talk', I discovered that among the things Aunt Marie did at the convent were: climbing up to peep at the nuns when they were bathing; carving little statues of them from soap; hiding pieces of meat and meaty bones in her skirt pockets whenever they had soup for lunch. Soup, apparently, was a regular part of the girls' diet but the nuns never allowed them to eat the meat or suck the bones. They had to leave them at the sides of their plates for the piggy barrel, though I suppose this was more to restrain the girls from

---

assuaged soothed
prostrate lying down

making pigs of themselves, rather than for the benefit of the pigs.

Nevertheless, Aunt Marie grew up to be a staunch Catholic, attending all the different masses and church meetings and saying all her Hail Marys.

One of her favourite saints was Saint Anthony, the patron saint for finding things. Since she was a bit absent-minded and was always losing things, you could see why she liked him. Most of the times we visited her she was bound to misplace something or other, especially her spectacles which she left in the oddest of places. She would go around saying her little prayer which went something like this: 'Saint Anthony, perfect imitator of Jesus, Restorer of lost things, grant that I may find my ...'

It never failed to work as after a short while she would exclaim triumphantly, 'Saint Anthony is good. Saint Anthony is really, really good.' I couldn't help wondering what her reaction would be if Saint Anthony turned a deaf ear on her just once in a while.

I got the chance one day when she was visiting and left her handbag lying half-opened in a corner of our living room floor. Peeping out at the top were the blue glassy beads of her rosary. I pulled it out and waited impatiently for her to discover the loss. First I asked if she had a pencil to lend me, then a pen. She said no to both and didn't even bother to look in her handbag. Then a friend of mine came across to play and I soon forgot all about Aunt Marie and her rosary.

It was only when she was ready to leave that Aunt Marie discovered the loss. Her shrieking made me rush upstairs.

'Girl, you know anything about your Aunt Marie's rosary?' my mother asked, searching my face suspiciously. I denied knowing. Aunt Marie's face was flushed and angry. Instead of going round muttering her usual prayer to Saint Anthony as I was hoping, she was getting more and more worked up about it, especially when my mother suggested she might have left it at home. At this point Aunt Marie was clutching her bag, so I couldn't slip the rosary back in.

As soon as my mother left the room I got the rosary and quickly threw it through the half open doorway where Aunt Marie, short, plumpish and breathing heavily, was standing.

It landed at her feet with a small clatter on the wooden floor.

Aunt Marie snatched it up then fell dramatically on her knees, clutching the necklace of blue beads and vowing vehemently, 'To God, Edna, I am not coming back to your house. I am not coming back. Let the Virgin Mary be my witness.'

It was the longest time that Aunt Marie ever stayed away from our house – a whole week.

But it was with some relief that I heard her voice floating up the stairs that morning, 'O God, Edna, a cup-of-tea, a cup-of-tea, the wind, the wind.'

The Tiger Ladies, a Memoir of Kashmir
by *Sudha Koul*

In these two extracts, the first descriptive and the second narrative, the writer shares the fondness she feels for her grandmother. These passages also show that young people often have similar experiences, however different their cultural backgrounds. As you read these two extracts you should focus upon:
- the language the writer uses to express her regard and affection for her grandmother
- the way in which the writer explores her relationship with her grandmother rather than just telling us about it.

Sudha Koul was brought up as a Hindu, in a predominantly Muslim valley in Kashmir. She was born in 1947, the year when the country was divided into India and Pakistan. Despite the political problems, she recalls an idyllic childhood.

My grandmother, Dhanna, has a mouth that smells like babies, all milky, toothless, and harmless, except when she smokes her hookah. She of the crisply washed cotton dress dried on the grass in the sun; her clothes smell of the herbs of spring and summer, and of the earth; she makes buttermilk drinks all day. Dhanna sits there at her kitchen window, one knee on the seasoned sill, the other knee balancing a round metal pot in which she whips up buttermilk flavoured with salt and dried mint powder. I watch her make white and green foam as she churns the wooden whisk between her cracked dry palms.

The mint is from her grandfather's well. The leaves are plucked, then washed and dried on the wood-shingled rooftop. When the mint is so dry that it crumbles to the touch, it is powdered by a small round stone mortar in an oval pestle, both of which have blackened with use and time.

'The well water is so pure that it makes the leaves fragrant,' says my mother's mother, Dhanna. 'You must have mint buttermilk drinks in summer. It cools everything.' She says, although she drinks glasses of her concoction even in winter because she thinks women must always have buttermilk or yogurt. But in the summer she churns the sweet **elixir** all day, and offers it to everyone who walks in her wooden door, bending a little as they enter her well-worn portal.

* * *

Dhanna and I are chasing the sun round the house, moving our chairs every half hour or so. Like other children in my family I call my grandparents by their names. She leans forward and feels the cartilage inside my upper earlobe, the area from which the wedding ornaments are going to be worn.

She says once again, 'Your ears are ready for piercing; your mother must get it done now.'

There is a note of pessimism in my grandmother's voice because she knows that if it was going to be done it would have been done much earlier, when the cartilage in the upper ear is as soft as it is in the lower lobe. She knows that my other grandfather's house is modern, and that I will probably never get my upper ears pierced; too many from my family have spent too many years in other parts of India where people live very different lives. She is filled with compassion for her poor daughter and granddaughter.

---

elixir a medicinal or magical drink

She says almost inaudibly, mainly to herself, 'Where will you string your wedding ornaments if your upper ears are not ready? You cannot hang them over your ears like a horse.'

She sees me as a smaller version of herself. She has had her Sikh jeweller with the intoxicated eyes fashion miniature versions of her gigantic gold wire hoops for me. I wear my child earrings in the unmarried part of my ear lobes, and she loves to see me wear the jewellery she orders for me.

'Look how pretty you look,' she says, smiling proudly.

She holds my earrings between her thumb and forefinger and gently pulls them, and me, close to her eyes as she checks the quality of the workmanship for the umpteenth time, but her thoughts are on my unpierced upper earlobes and my unpreparedness. She smiles at me as if I am deaf and dumb and have no idea of the foolishness of my modern parents.

Wild Swans
by *Jung Chang*

The strength of the writer's love for her grandmother, who suffered the painful experience of foot binding, is revealed through the powerful language and structure in this extract. The reader is also given moving insights into a very different culture. As you read this extract you should focus upon:

- the way that structure within and between paragraphs has been used for particular effects
- the writer's powerful, emotive use of language.

Wild Swans is the memoir of three generations of a family: the writer, her mother and her grandmother. It tells the history of China through most of the twentieth century from a female perspective. Much of what she has to say is upsetting and disturbing, but this extract reveals the tremendous regard the writer feels for her grandmother as well as her criticism of the traditional practice of foot binding.

My grandmother was a beauty. She had an oval face, with rosy cheeks and lustrous skin. Her long, shiny black hair was woven into a thick plait reaching down to her waist. She could be demure when the occasion demanded, which was most of the time, but underneath her composed exterior she was bursting with suppressed energy. She was petite, about five feet three inches, with a slender figure and sloping shoulders, which were considered the ideal.

But her greatest assets were her bound feet, called in Chinese 'three-inch golden lilies' (*san-tsun-gin-lian*). This meant she walked 'like a tender young willow shoot in a spring breeze,' as Chinese connoisseurs of women traditionally put it.

My grandmother's feet had been bound when she was two years old. Her mother, who herself had bound feet, first wound a piece of white cloth about twenty feet long round her feet, bending all the toes except the big toe inwards and under the sole. Then she placed a large stone on top to crush the arch. My grandmother screamed in agony and begged her to stop. Her mother had to stick a cloth into her mouth to gag her. My grandmother passed out repeatedly from the pain.

The process lasted several years. Even after the bones had been broken, the feet had to be bound day and night in thick cloth because the moment they were released they would try to recover. For years my grandmother lived in relentless, excruciating pain. When she pleaded with her mother to untie the bindings, her mother would weep and tell her that unbound feet would ruin her entire life, and that she was doing it for her own future happiness.

In those days, when a woman was married, the first thing the bridegroom's family did was to examine her feet. Large feet, meaning normal feet, were considered to bring shame on the husband's household. The mother-in-law would lift the hem of the bride's long skirt, and if the feet were more than about four inches long, she would throw down the skirt in a demonstrative gesture of contempt and stalk off, leaving the bride to the critical gaze of the wedding guests, who would stare at her feet and insultingly mutter their disdain. Sometimes a mother would take pity on her daughter and remove the binding cloth; but when the child grew up and had to endure the contempt of her husband's family and the disapproval of society, she would blame her mother for having been too weak.

Women could not remove the binding cloths even when they were adults, as their feet would start growing again. The binding would only be loosened temporarily at night in bed, when they would put on soft-soled shoes. Men rarely saw naked bound feet, which were usually covered in rotting flesh and stank when the bindings were removed. As a child, I can remember my grandmother being in constant pain. When we came home from shopping, the first thing she would do was soak her feet in a bowl of hot water, sighing with relief as she did so. Then she would set about cutting off pieces of dead skin. The pain came not only from the broken bones, but also from her toenails, which grew into the balls of her feet.

In fact, my grandmother's feet were bound just at the moment when foot-binding was disappearing for good. By the time her sister was born in 1917, the practice had virtually been abandoned, so she escaped the torment.

A Middle Eastern Affair
by *Claudia Roden*

This extract is interesting because the writer's feelings for the place are evident in the sounds, rhythms and images evoked through her choice of language. As you read this extract you should focus upon:
- the way the writer uses language to show her love of Egyptian food and festivals
- the way the writer uses paragraph and sentence structure to convey her feelings.

The writer is famous for books about food and this extract comes from the introduction to a section in one of her cookery books. Through her writing, we are able to share her love of food even without following her recipes.

Some of my happiest childhood memories are of picnics in Egypt. My favourite was on the dunes of Agami in Alexandria. It was timed to coincide with the arrival of migrating quails on the beaches. The birds fell exhausted, to be caught in large nets and collected in baskets. They were cleaned and marinated in a rich cumin and coriander sauce and grilled on the beach over small fires. Fresh Arab bread was bought from the vendors who sang their wares on the beaches and played odds and even for a handful of pistachios or peanuts. The hollow rounds of bread were cut in half, opened out and placed under the birds to catch their flavoursome juices; then the quails were gathered in them to be eaten as a sandwich, soft bones and all. Water-melons and pieces of coconut and sweet nutty pastries, bought from the vendors, ended the meal.

Another popular picnic spot was near a small dam we called simply 'le barrage'. We would bring large quantities of ful medames (Egyptian brown beans) in giant saucepans, on top if which were embedded shelled eggs which had been boiled gently for many hours with onion skins until they became light brown and their yolks creamy. A large box lined with foil held a salad of coarsely chopped tomatoes, cucumbers, cos lettuce, spring onions with parsley and fresh coriander leaves.

The beans were warmed up over a primus stove while we unrolled our rugs and settled down in expectation of the 'gala-gala', a magician who invariably produced baby chicks out of metal cups and eggs out of noses. We filled pouches of bread with the beans and sprinkled them with olive oil and a squeeze of lemon. Some people liked to add a crushed clove of garlic. We placed an egg cut in four in each portion, pressed down the beans and topped them with salad. A basket of fruit was followed by a variety of pastries filled with pistachio nuts, almonds, walnuts and dates, scented lightly with rose water and orange blossom water.

In an area which harbours many of nomadic ancestry and over which the sun shines constantly, eating out is a way of life. There are even official occasions for picnics.

Amongst these are the 'mulids' when people flock to the principle scenes of religious festivals, public gardens, shrines, tombs of saints and burial grounds. Thousands gather sometimes for days and nights, sleeping under tents. Dervishes perform and itinerant entertainers recite ancient romances of unrequited love and 'crime passionnel'. Conjurers no longer astonish with their age old tricks but people watch enthralled. They laugh at the buffoons and admire the acrobat's skill with the same pleasure that children have in listening to the same bed-time stories for years, noticing every little addition and new twist to the plot. Stick dancers, white robes flowing and turbans swaying, simulate a fight. Food is prepared for the whole period of the festival. It can be supplemented from the numerous stalls, erected with the swings and whirligigs, which sell falafels, kebabs, pastries and sweetmeats and stay open all night, lit up by lanterns. When the festival is over and the tents and stalls are taken down, cracked egg shells, dyed red or yellow to bring joy and happiness, limp lettuce leaves and discarded empty melon seeds carpet the area of activity.

The most important of the national picnics in Egypt is not a religious occasion. It is Shem en Nesseem, which celebrates the arrival of spring. Town dwellers go out in the country or in boats, generally northwards, eating out in the fields or on the river bank, smelling the air which is thought to be particularly beneficial on that day.

But no one waits for an official occasion.

In the **Levant** a picnic is not for the silent enjoyment of nature. You are too busy and too merry to notice the sea, the mountain or the river bank. The rule is the larger the group the better the picnic. The more for backgammon and cards. The more there are to tell jokes, the wealthier the gossip. The more there are that will sing and dance and the more dishes to choose from.

Few occasions can satisfy at the same time the convivial Arab spirit, the pleasure of being entertained and the legendary hospitality, as a picnic does. You are generous host and joyous guest at the same time, and the ultimate aim, to please, is developed to the point of an art in the contents of the picnic basket.

Levant the eastern Mediterranean

Activities

Spaghetti Bolognese

The writer relates events in an amusing way by recreating the events and characters through his lively use of language and his choice of dialogue. Explore how he does this by completing the tasks below.

1 A variety of lively words is used instead of *says*. For example, Dad *snaps*. Make a list of the words that are used to describe the way each character speaks. What do we learn about them and the situation from the way they speak?

  a Look at the dialogue in the first paragraph. What makes this an entertaining opening?

  b Before the spaghetti is cooked, it is described as *spikes* and *brittle sticks*, but after cooking, it is said to be *escaping* and *curling*. Find two more examples that describe the spaghetti before it is cooked and after it is cooked. Why are they effective?

  c Because spaghetti bolognese is unfamiliar to the family, the writer uses similes (comparisons using the words *like* or *as*) to describe it. He says that the strands of cooked spaghetti were *curling up in the sink like nests of worms*. Find two more similes and explain why each is effective.

  d Read the final, very short paragraph. What makes this paragraph funny?

2 Pick your three favourite humorous moments from the extract. Write each one in the centre of a page and annotate it to show why you have chosen it. For example:

Suggests Dad is unfamiliar with cooking pasta and conveys his uncertainty.

Far too long to cook spaghetti; tells us Dad doesn't know what he is doing and we laugh at his ignorance.

Simile makes eating spaghetti seem as unfamiliar and unpleasant as eating worms; 'nest of worms' echoes the idea of a 'nest of vipers', suggesting hidden dangers.

'I think it must be done now,' says my father twenty minutes later. He drains the slithery lengths of spaghetti in a colander in the sink. Some are escaping through the holes and curling up in the sink like a nest of worms. 'Quick, get the plates, they're getting away.'

The word 'slithery' is onomatopoeic and suggests how strange the spaghetti feels.

Spaghetti personified when the word 'escaping' is used; suggests that it's a strange and uncontrollable enemy getting the better of Dad.

Dad's sharp order suggests he cannot control the spaghetti.

Use of commas in final sentence helps break up the sentence and make it sound disjointed and panicky.

Continues the personification of the spaghetti strands and builds on the idea that it's too difficult to control.

Cider with Rosie

1 The writer makes skilful use of language and other literary features to create an affectionate, humorous picture of his mother. Explore how he does this by completing the tasks below.

   a The extract gives an impression of chaos. What can you find to suggest that this confusion is quite normal in this household?

   b The writer uses lists to suggest confusion. Find **two** of them and and write them out.

   c Count how many things are going wrong or are being done in an unconventional way. What is the effect of mentioning so many?

   d We are told that breakfast will *presently emerge*. What does the word *emerge* tell us about how much control Mother has over the breakfast preparations?

   e At the end of the extract, Mother complains that if she had a *proper stove* things would be different. Do you believe what she says? Give reasons for your answer.

2 Comment on the writer's feelings for his mother. He shows us the morning muddle, but he does not criticise her for her lack of organisation. How does he create an affectionate picture of her and the chaos in which she lives? In your answer you should consider:

   • words and phrases that suggest that confusion was the norm
   • the use of lists to suggest that many things were happening at the same time
   • suggestions that everyday things were being done in unconventional ways
   • Mother's **ineffectual** comments.

---

ineffectual not making any difference to the situation

3 Think of the most chaotic family that you know. In no more than three paragraphs, describe the morning muddle in this house. Remember:

- that you are allowed to exaggerate the facts
- to create a vivid but affectionate picture of the main character
- to use lists
- to include some dialogue that reveals character.

Bad Blood

1 Copy out or put a sheet of acetate/tracing paper over the table on the next page. Draw lines to join the techniques for creating humour with the appropriate examples and additional comments.

2 Consider carefully how the writer makes her work entertaining. Using some of her techniques, rewrite the very dull piece of writing below in a more entertaining way. You may make up extra details if you wish.

My father was very well organised. For many years he worked in a factory where his job was to check in all the supplies that arrived in the factory and also to keep a tally of everything that left on the various trucks and lorries.

At home, he liked everything to be as organised as it was at work. He wrote all the shopping lists with very great care and checked all the food that was in the cupboards and the fridge. He liked meals to be regular and if he didn't get the food he expected on each night of the week he made a fuss.

Father insisted that everything was in the right place, including the contents of our bedrooms.

Even after we paid for him to go to a therapist to learn how to relax, he still came home and complained that our shoes were not polished and lined up in the right order in the hall.

Techniques for creating humour	Examples from the text	Additional comments
The writer uses personification (giving human characteristics to non-living things).	*I can still recall my mother's recipe for lumpy gravy.*	These words create an amusing, vivid picture of how bad the food was, cooked for so long that it became far too soft or was burnt.
The writer uses interesting onomatopoeic (sounding like their meanings) nouns and verbs.	*For instance, ham and tongue cut into see-through slices; sandwiches of meat-paste or fish-paste or bananas; canned corned beef, luncheon meat (Spam in civilian clothes), pilchards, sardines, salmon, baked beans and spaghetti; tinned peaches, pears and plums, and fruit salad with mauve 'cherries' and condensed milk.*	Here the writer agrees that there can be few problems with baked beans and then is amused to find that her mother still finds a way of spoiling them. This effect is increased by the writer's use of conversational language – *(say)* and *True …* which makes her sound resigned and unbothered by her mother's failings.
The writer uses irony (saying one thing and meaning another).	*… but there wasn't a lot that could go wrong with (say) baked beans on toast. True, the beans were stewed (with extra water) to be on the safe side.*	It is ironic to suggest that her mother needed a recipe to make such bad gravy. The use of the word *recipe* also makes us think that she always did the same thing as if this was the proper way to do it.
The writer uses lists to suggest number and variety.	*… she thought vegetables even more dangerous and difficult to subdue. … nature was grandly snubbed and outdone.'*	Such a long list reveals the delight that the family felt at being given food that needed no cooking. The writer calls it a *rich list*. The effect is heightened when she goes on to mention more convenience foods which she calls their *staple diet*.
The writer surprises the reader by drawing attention to problems when the reader had begun to believe that no problems remained.	*mush, sludge, frazzled*	This exaggerates Mother's inability to deal with vegetables, making them sound as if they were deliberately refusing to cook properly. Similarly, nature is seen as an enemy with whom Mother fought but who was finally beaten by the introduction of convenience foods.

My Place – Wolverhampton

1 Look carefully at the extract to see how the writer has used both language and structure to express his thoughts about the place in which he lives. Clearly this text is written by a teenager. This is evident both from the subject matter and from the language used. What does he write about that would concern teenagers? Find words that you would associate with young people.

2 The fourth, fifth and sixth paragraphs describe the Generation club night. Which words, phrases or sentences do you think best convey the atmosphere of the evening? Choose **three** quotations and explain your choice.

3 Find an example of each of the following devices that the writer uses to show his enthusiasm for Wolverhampton:

- contrast with ideas the reader might already have about Wolverhampton, for example, that nothing happens there
- use of lists
- use of repeated words at the beginnings of phrases, for example in the fifth paragraph
- use of enthusiastic vocabulary.

4 Look at the way the article has been planned and structured.

a Give each of the eight paragraphs a title.

b Explain how the last paragraph links back to the first paragraph.

c How does the second paragraph link with the first?

d How does the last sentence of the second paragraph prepare the reader for the first sentence of the third paragraph?

e The middle of the article is about just one evening. Why has the writer chosen to write about that evening?

5 In pairs, discuss how you might write enthusiastically about your own home area. Draw up a plan and discuss the vocabulary and language devices you might use. Suggest a structure or plan for your writing. Then write your own essay.

Remembering Aunt Marie

The writer manipulates both structure and language to make her story lively and entertaining. Explore how she does this by answering the questions below.

1 It is interesting that the first paragraph is about respect. What is it about Aunt Marie that you might not find conventionally respectable?

2 a Think about the character of Aunt Marie and how the writer feels about her. Look at the following examples of the kinds of things Aunt Marie says:

- *O God, Edna, a cup-of-tea, a cup-of-tea, the wind, the wind.*
- *O God, the bunions, my name ain't Marie if it don't rain.*
- *Saint Anthony is good. Saint Anthony is really, really good.*

What do we learn about her character from what she says and from the way she says it?

b Look carefully at the paragraph that begins 'Aunt Marie snatched it up…'. Which verbs and adverbs from this paragraph make Aunt Marie sound particularly frantic?

c Compare the things that Aunt Marie did when she was a girl with the writer's joke with the rosary. What do the two of them have in common?

d How do the writer's language choices show that she was fond of Aunt Marie?

3 With a partner, improvise a situation where Aunt Marie is telling another family friend about the incident with the rosary. You should ensure that you show:

- an understanding of how Aunt Marie speaks
- an understanding of what Aunt Marie believed had happened
- an appreciation of Aunt Marie's feelings for the writer and her family.

4 We are told a little about Aunt Marie's appearance, but we can imagine a good deal more. Either:

a Draw Aunt Marie to show how her appearance and clothing might reflect her character and annotate your drawing to explain your decisions, or

b Write a full description of how you imagine that she looks and dresses and explain your choices by referring to the text.

The Tiger Ladies, A Memoir of Kashmir

1 In the first extract, the writer chooses particular memories to express her fondness for her grandmother, Dhanna. Complete the table below to show your understanding of how she reveals this affection.

Point	Example/quotation	Comment
smells pleasant	*Dhanna has a mouth that smells like babies, all milky, toothless and harmless.*	Uses a simile that compares her with something sweet and lovable; adjectives all suggest that Dhanna is incapable of hurting her
old fashioned and traditional		
associated with pleasant, natural things		
takes care of her granddaughter and performs motherly, nurturing tasks		

Point	Example/quotation	Comment
indulgent towards her granddaughter		
can be relied upon always to do the same things at the same time in the same way		

2 In the second extract, it is Dhanna's feelings about her granddaughter having her ears pierced and the relationship between them that are important.

   a How does the writer convey her grandmother's concern and the strength of their relationship?

   b Pick out **two** quotations that show that Dhanna and her grandaughter are very close – almost the same person.

   c Which words show that the matter of the earrings has been on Dhanna's mind for a long time and that she cannot get it out of her head?

3 The use of speech is an important way of bringing the character of Dhanna to life. Look again at the things she says. Does she talk about herself and her own feelings by using the word *I*, or does she talk about Sudha using the word *you*? What does this tell us about her?

4 The writer uses the present tense (*Dhanna <u>has</u> a mouth*). What difference does this make to how vivid her descriptions seem?

5 Think of an older person to whom you have been close. Write a description of that person and then relate an incident that explores your relationship with them. Try to include the following features:

   • description of appearance and things normally done
   • the present tense
   • speech to show the closeness of the relationship.

Wild Swans

1 The writer uses both language and the structure of her text to convey her feelings about her grandmother's beauty and her experience of foot binding.

a Look carefully at the first paragraph of the extract. This is a good example of a paragraph beginning with a topic sentence which is then exemplified in the rest of the paragraph. List all the things mentioned in the paragraph that add up to the grandmother being considered beautiful.

b The second paragraph tells us how foot binding was meant to make women appear delicate and charming, while the third and fourth paragraphs show us how painful and ugly the practice really was. Choose quotations to show this contrast. Write them in a table like the one below.

Delicate	Painful and ugly
three-inch golden lilies	*screamed in agony*

2 What is the effect of juxtaposing (setting side by side) the idea that foot binding made women appear delicate and beautiful and the fact that it was a painful, ugly practice?

a In the fifth paragraph, the writer uses a number of words meaning to dislike or not approve. Find as many of these words as you can. What is the effect of using a variety of words for the same thing?

b A bride's new in-laws might expect her feet to have been bound, but in the sixth and seventh paragraphs the writer relates her own personal memories of her grandmother's feet. What makes this more moving than simply writing her opinions of foot binding?

3 Use your answers to the questions above to help you explain how the writer creates such a powerful picture of her grandmother. Remember to write about both language and structure and to refer closely to the text by using quotations.

A Middle Eastern Affair

1 Work in pairs. One of you should write step-by-step instructions for preparing the meal eaten at Agami. The other should write instructions for preparing the picnic eaten at the dam they called *le barrage*.

   a When you are finished, discuss which of the picnics you would prefer. Give reasons for your choice. Compare these picnics with other experiences of eating outdoors that you have enjoyed.

2 Look at the fifth paragraph, where the *mulids* or religious festivals are described. Here the writer creates a sense of activity and excitement by:

- using words that suggest that there are large numbers of people present
- repeatedly giving the name of a kind of performer at the beginning of the sentence and then going on to describe what they do using imaginative verbs
- using lists to imply abundance and variety
- using compound sentences containing *and* to give the impression that there are many things going on.

Find at least two examples to support each of the bullet points.

3 In the extract there is a one-sentence paragraph. Explain why this is effective here.

4 Look at the eighth paragraph. Which words are repeated at the beginning of sentences to give a feeling of conviviality (of everyone being welcome and getting on well together)?

5 Think of a time when you have enjoyed eating outside in lively surroundings. Write a descriptive account. You could consider:

- hot pies at a football match
- candy floss and toffee apples at a fairground
- fast food at a theme park.

Use some of the writer's ideas to create a sense of excitement in your own writing.

Comparing the extracts

The extracts in this section give different perspectives on similar subject matter. The activities below ask you to draw some comparisons between the texts in terms of:

- their purpose
- their audience
- the way the writing is crafted according to purpose and audience
- the impact and significance the writing has on you as a reader.

The final discussion activity asks you to make some judgements about the qualities of each of the extracts in this section and to draw your own conclusions about whether they are *literary* non-fiction.

1 Look at the three extracts about bad cooks by Laurie Lee, Lorna Sage and Nigel Slater. Which of the three parents – Mrs Lee, Mrs Sage or Mr Slater – would you least like to cook for you? Give reasons for your answer.

2 Imagine going to share a meal cooked by one of them. You may choose the meal. Write an account of your visit, making your writing as vibrant as you can by using some of the techniques employed by the writers in this section.

3 *Remembering Aunt Marie* is about a person. *My Place – Wolverhampton* describes a place. Both are about something we might not look upon favourably – Aunt

Marie and Wolverhampton – but which the writers describe in an enthusiastic way. Both have a similar structure in that they start by describing the place or person in general and then go on to relate a particular event. Choose an unattractive character or place from life, a soap opera, film or play and describe him, her, or it in an affectionate way using a similar structure.

4 The extract by Jung Chang is about foot binding and the one by Sudha Koul is about ear piercing. In both pieces, the writers' views are **implicit**. Teenagers in Britain today sometimes have disagreements with adults about making permanent changes to their bodies by having tattoos, cosmetic surgery, or body piercing. Write a speech for a debate either for or against the motion:
Young people should have the freedom to do as they please with their own bodies.

In your speech, you should refer to one or both of the extracts that you have read.

5 Having read all of the extracts in this section, decide which one of the writers you can relate to most closely. Choose three or four moments from that extract and explain how or why this is similar to an aspect of your own life.

6 In working through these extracts, you have explored a range of features that make them distinctive. All of the extracts are about things that have really happened, so they all belong with non-fiction rather than fiction; the crucial question is, are they *literary* non-fiction?

In small groups, working on a copy of the grid on page 199, review each of the texts and decide which of the criteria for literary non-fiction each one meets. Then decide which extracts are definitely literary non-fiction and which ones you are less confident about. Be prepared to share your judgements. Remember that there are no right and wrong answers!

---

implicit implied but not actually said

Section 2

Dramatic moments: experiencing the feelings of a writer

This section looks at exciting events and adventures where the writer involves the reader in the tension and drama. While reading the extracts, it might be helpful to keep the following questions in mind.

- What is revealed of these especially courageous characters?
- How much are we told directly about the characters and their situations and how much is implied?
- How do the writers involve their readers in the excitement and adventure by their manipulation of language and structure?

Extracts in this section

1 *In Black and White* by Donald McRae
2 *The Cruellest Miles* by Gay and Laney Salisbury
3 *Amy Johnson, Queen of the Air* by Midge Gillies
4 *Terra Incognita, Travels in Antarctica* by Sara Wheeler
5 *A Covered Wagon Girl* by Sallie Hester
6 *Don't Let's Go to the Dogs Tonight* by Alexandra Fuller

Why the extracts have been selected

Extracts 1–3 are all races of some sort. They are exciting and full of tension because the writers convey the drama of the events to the readers. In all three extracts, the writers also set out to inform the reader. Extract 1 has a more educational purpose about race and history.

Extracts 4–6 are about people striking out to achieve what is necessary. The way the writers convey the feelings, character and courage of the central figures is important. Extract 4 is a piece of travel writing that draws out similarities with an earlier famous explorer. Extract 5 is a diary – a personal account that was written not for publication, but to inform and record events. Extract 6 is an autobiography where the writer sets out both to relate an event and to entertain the reader.

In Black and White
by *Donald McRae*

In this extract the writer relates an exciting sporting and significant political event in a dramatic way. As you read this extract you should focus upon:
- the language the writer uses to make this account dramatic
- the way in which the sentence and paragraph structures help to create tension
- the way in which the writing is crafted to affect the feelings of the reader.

In Black and White *is about the success of two black American sportsmen, Joe Louis and Jesse Louis. Jesse Owens, the subject of this extract, won four gold medals in the Berlin Olympics of August 1936, striking out not for just himself and his country but for all black people, who were despised by Hitler and the Nazis.*

Late the following afternoon, at 4.55, the rainy cold made Jesse shiver as he stripped down to his vest and shorts for the 100m final – the most prestigious event of the entire Olympiad and the defining moment of his life. Hitler was once more in his box, hoping that **Borchmeyer** might somehow defeat the Negro sprinters and win the title of the World's Fastest Man for Nazi Germany.

Jesse had spent the morning resting on the small bed **Larry Snyder** had set up for him in their dressing-room. Just after 12.30 p.m. he ate the cold steak sandwiches and drank the milk and the coffee Snyder had brought for him

---

Borchmeyer a German athlete
Larry Snyder Jesse Owens' coach

in two Thermos flasks. Three hours later he won the first semi-final, streaking away from **Wykoff** and **Hans Strandberg** of Sweden. The damp and scuffed **cinder** felt heavy beneath his feet, even if he seemed to run as effortlessly as ever. Jesse's time, comparatively slow for him at 10.3, reflected the deterioration of the track. He had already lost his world record from the day before, having been informed that his 'wind-assisted' 10.2 in the quarter-final had been ruled inadmissible. Jesse didn't care about breaking the record. He just wanted gold.

Ralph Metcalfe was equally determined. He won the second semi-final in 10.5 which meant that, of the six finalists, only he and Owens had yet to lose a race in Berlin. His ambition was deepened by the disappointment he had suffered in the 1942 Olympic final. Metcalfe was convinced that he, rather than Eddie Tolan, should have been given the gold medal after they finished in a virtual dead-heat. If the twenty-two-year-old Owens still had the 200m and the long jump to come, and perhaps other Games in the future, the 100m final offered Metcalfe his last chance of an Olympic win.

Owens, in the inside lane, clasped his hands in front of his face when his name was announced first. He thought of Charley Riley as he looked down at the length of the track. He could hear Pop's words in his head, as if they were back in Cleveland staring at the concrete alley which ran alongside the old black church: *'Imagine you're sprinting over a ground of burning fire.'*

At 4.58 the six men dug their foot-holds in the cinder. Silence descended over the Olympic stadium. The crowd scanned the runners as they lined up alongside each other. Owens, Strandberg, Borchmeyer, Osendarp,

---

Wykoff, Hans Strandberg athletes
cinder small pieces of partly burnt wood or coal, used to surface running tracks

Wykoff and Metcalfe. Hitler leaned forward excitedly, his right fist banging lightly against the railing.

Jesse Owens knew that ten seconds would determine the outcome of eight years of dedicated training. He crouched down and placed his fingers just behind the white line. He stretched out his legs to find the holes he had just dug with his trowel.

The starter's soothing voice steadied Owens' twitching legs. *'Auf die Plätze...'*

Owens lifted his head. His eyes misted in concentration as he stared at the finish line. *'Fertig!'*

Owens raised himself from his haunches. His mind went blank.

The gun cracked loud and flat in the immense stillness.

Owens was out of the holes first. The sound of the others, and of the suddenly roaring crowd, dropped away. He was surrounded by silence once more. Owens was lost to the world. He was already racing. He was flying. With his head held high and almost perfectly still, his arms and legs blurred inside their rhythmic pumping. His feet, as always, barely seemed to touch the track.

Owens had opened up a clear lead after thirty metres, ahead of Strandberg and Osendarp with Metcalfe trailing badly after an appalling start. In the adjoining lane, and already a metre down, Strandberg clawed at a muscle in his leg as if he could no longer stand the strain of racing Owens. The Swedish sprinter kept running but Owens glided further ahead, sweeping soundlessly through the halfway mark. With Osendarp now second, Metcalfe began to impose himself. He powered past the outclassed Borchmeyer and the grimacing Strandberg before closing on Wykoff.

Two metres in front, and with only twenty to run, the race belonged to Owens. He flew serenely towards the tape. Metcalfe, however, was now hurtling down the track, charging towards the finish as he moved into second place ahead of Osendarp. The gap between Metcalfe and Owens had narrowed to a metre, but it was too late. Owens snapped the tape and kept running, only slowing as he rounded the bend at the end of the straight. It had looked easy; but a sudden trembling ripped through him. He put his hands on his hips and began to breathe again, gulping fast and hard as he heard the now familiar chant: '*Yess-say ... Oh-vens ... Yess-say ... Oh-vens ...*'

When Jesse eventually stood on the winner's dais and looked up at the giant results board – *100m Lauf Männer Entscheidung: 1 Owens (USA) 10.3; 2 Metcalfe (USA) 10.4; 3 Osendarp (Holland) 10.5* – three blonde women approached the podium. Before Jesse received his gold medal, a laurel wreath was placed around his head while one of the women presented him with a small potted oak from the Black Forest, given to every winner as a gift from Germany. Jesse and Ralph stood to attention while the 'Stars and Stripes' resounded around the arena. The young German women turned to the American flag and lifted their arms in the Nazi salute.

The Cruellest Miles
by *Gay and Laney Salisbury*

This is an extract from a dramatic real-life adventure. A gripping mix of powerful language and facts gives the reader insights into the heroism of both humans and animals. As you read this extract you should focus upon:

- the way in which the writers give the facts in order to build up tension
- the use of powerful, direct language and sentence structures to heighten the drama
- the writers' skill in bringing the characters to life.

The gold-rush town of Nome is situated in Alaska, just below the Arctic Circle. In 1925, suffering an outbreak of diphtheria, the people of the town desperately needed medicine. However, the port was icebound, the nearest railway was almost 700 miles away across mountains, rivers and treacherous ice, and aeroplanes had not yet been tested in such conditions. The only way to get the serum to the town was to take it by a relay of dog sleds in a thrilling race against time. This extract tells of the journey from Nenana (where the railway met the mail trail to Nome) along the Tanana River. Shannon was the 'musher' or leader of the dog sled team.

Satisfied that everything was in order, Shannon mounted the runners, released the sled, and took off, bolting along the tracks, down the bank to the Tanana River and into the cold, dark Interior. He had never had such a large audience watch him start a run, but tonight there was no time to think about anything but the job ahead.

High above the endless spires of spruce and birch, the stars shone with cold brilliance and the moon was silver in the sky, less than a quarter full.

The route would follow the Tanana River northwards in three long meandering curves for the thirty miles to Minto, an Athabaskan village in the lowlands, and then curve sharply to the west to Tolovana. It was a varied terrain of smooth surfaces and upended pieces of ice that could bruise the knees and break elbows, and the trail often required heavy pushing and frustrating lurches.

As they crossed the Tanana to the trail on the east bank, the dogs surged forward in their collars, panting heavily and leaving behind wisps of steam that hung for a moment like ghosts along the trail. On any other occasion, the veils would have been beautiful to watch, but on that evening they were a sign that the dogs were moving too fast in the severe cold. In addition, the route was in atrocious shape. A few days earlier, a horse team dragging heavy freight had punched deep holes in the trail. For years, the horse teams had been the bane of the dog rigs.

Shannon's team fought to keep its footing, but finally Shannon accepted that the trail was too broken up to be of use. Shouting, 'Haw!' he ordered Blackie to turn left and lead the team onto the Tanana River. The temperature would be several degrees colder on the frozen river than on the steep bank but at least the path had not been broken up by the horses.

Shannon was taking a big risk. In any type of weather, travelling over a frozen river can be extremely dangerous. River ice is in a constant state of transformation. It can be smooth along one stretch and a jumble of craggy ice sculptures on the next. The large frozen peaks are strong enough to support a truck, but the narrow valleys in between can easily crack underfoot.

It was nearly pitch dark, and though Shannon was fighting the numbing cold, he had managed to stay alert, and was watching for hazards along the river. He was particularly worried about overflow, a phenomenon that can occur in any type of winter weather, but which at 50 degrees below is life-threatening. Overflow occurs when water bursts through the surface and seeps over the top of the ice. The pent-up water can be under such pressure that it forms a geyser sometimes three or four feet high and the slick may spread for miles across the ice.

In warmer weather, many sled dogs love to splash through overflow, but in temperatures below zero a dog will do his best to avoid it. If a team drives through overflow in the bitter cold, a driver must stop immediately, cut down boughs of spruce, and build a fire to dry his moccasins and socks. A delay could cost him his toes, his foot, or his life.

It is also important to dry off each dog's paws, because the ice could build up and grind away at the pads, eventually crippling the animal. It was a cold and time-consuming operation that required working without gloves, but it was an absolute necessity. 'A man is only as good as his dogs when he is on the trails of Alaska ... and a dog is only as good as his feet,' a well-travelled dog driver once said.

Overflow refreezes quite rapidly, forming a fragile shell that will crack loudly or flex like rubber underfoot, either of which are clear signals for the traveller to get off. But once the overflow has completely frozen to a hard sheen, it can be as slippery as glass and unyielding to any toehold.

The other risk of riding over frozen rivers was what had been described as drum ice, the opposite of overflow. This threat was the greater of the two: while a good lead dog could avoid overflow, he was often unable to detect drum ice in time to avoid catastrophe. Drum ice occurs when the water beneath a frozen river recedes, leaving behind a deep ice cavern. It appears quite ordinary on the surface, but when a team drives over it the sled begins to make a hollow sound, like a drum. If the team doesn't get off quickly the ice could cave in and the driver fall 10 to 20 feet down to the dry riverbed.

Either way, it would be important for Shannon to remain calm: if he panicked, the dogs were likely to sense it and become unnerved, and this would only worsen the situation.

So far, Shannon had been lucky. His team had avoided any drum ice or overflow and the pups were working well together. But as the hours passed, a chill crept deeper into Shannon's bones. It was becoming harder and harder, he realised, to warm his extremities. He had to take immediate action and so began to swing his arms violently downwards at the same time that he began to pedal more frequently on the runners, hoping to drive the blood back into his fingers and toes. Then there was a gradual shift in perception. His focus began to move from the trail and the dogs to his own inability to stay warm.

Suddenly, Blackie made a sharp turn. The swing dogs followed in unison and the sled veered off. Shannon momentarily lost his balance but managed to hold onto the handlebars and regain his footing. Blackie's behaviour had been odd, was Shannon's first thought, until he was able to piece together what had happened: Blackie had avoided a black hole, an opening in the ice that had been eaten away by the current underneath and was 'large enough to drag down the entire team.'

Blackie had either seen the steam rising off the river or heard the rush of current against the hard-packed ice. He may have even felt the first vibration of cracking ice beneath his feet, for black holes have a tendency to widen quickly. Either way, he had reacted quickly. But something was wrong with four of the pups. Bear, Cub, Jack, and Jet were no longer running steadily. Sled dogs, at their best, will place their back leg inside the print of their forepaw, and many of them will be in step with each other. But as dogs tire, they fall out of rhythm. A pair of hind legs will be slow on the uptake. Another dog will begin crabbing, leaving paw prints at the edge of the trail as he stumbles, lags, and has to be dragged forward by the other dogs. Cub, Jack, and Jet were clearly exhausted. They had nothing left to draw on but heart, the sheer will to keep moving forward with the other dogs. And Bear was not much better. Shannon had been on the trail for four or five hours now. The temperature was still dropping and the colder it became, the slower time seemed to pass.

Shannon's own physical problems had not resolved themselves, and worse, his attempts to get blood down to his extremities no longer seemed to be paying off. If he did not do something quickly to get more heat to his legs, he knew what would happen. He would die, along with his dogs, and perishing with them would be any hope of getting the serum to Nome. His body was simply losing heat faster than he could produce it. In an attempt to protect against the cold, his body was shunting blood from its extremities to its core vital organs. Already his face was growing numb, and one of his big toes had become frozen. As sluggish as he felt, he knew what he had to do.

Shannon stopped the team and got off the sled. He raced to the front, just ahead of Blackie, and began to jog. The dogs matched their pace to Shannon's. When finally he felt the blood returning to his limbs, Shannon knew he had warmed up enough to go back to the sled and ride the runners.

This worked, but only for a while. Shannon was getting tired again, and, as he would recall, he was becoming 'fairly stupefied by the cold.'

Shannon was losing track of time. He forced himself to focus on Campbell's roadhouse in Minto, where he could warm up. As Shannon raced towards Minto, he was no doubt aware of the danger he and his dogs were in, but there was nothing he could do except thrash his arms against his sides, stomp his feet when he could, and continue to jog ahead of the dogs for short periods. When his extremities failed to warm up even after these attempts, he knew there was not enough heat in his core to spare. With the fear building inside him, he pushed on, knowing that he had to reach Minto before he lost control of himself and his team.

At around 3:00 A.M., the door to Johnny Campbell's roadhouse opened. Campbell took one look at Shannon and his dogs and it was clear to him that something terrible had happened. Parts of Shannon's face had turned black with severe frostbite. Blood had stained the mouths of Bear, Cub, Jack, and Jet. Helping Shannon inside, he placed him near the sheet-iron stove and poured him a cup of hot black coffee. Shannon was too tired and cold to eat. As he attempted the first sips of his coffee, he took a look at the thermometer outside: it was minus 62 degrees.

Amy Johnson, Queen of the Air
by *Midge Gillies*

This extract makes exciting reading because of the biographer's insights into the swiftly changing events. As you read this extract you should focus upon:
- the exciting, dramatic nature of the events themselves
- the writer's use of lively language
- the writer's use of imaginative similes and metaphors.

In May 1930, Amy Johnson, a typist from Hull, took off from Croydon Airport with a thermos flask and a packet of sandwiches, to try to beat the world solo record to Australia. She flew in a second-hand, open-cockpit biplane called Jason. *She had no radio communication and only the most basic of maps. The passage that follows recalls a forced landing in the Iraqi desert.*

Amy left Mouslimié at dawn. The desert was cold in first light and she zipped herself into her Sidcot flying suit before heading off in the direction of Baghdad some 500 miles south-east of Aleppo. She followed the twisting Euphrates river, where white 'beehive' houses made from mud-brick served as granaries, homes and stables. At times the steep, muddy river-banks merged into the surrounding landscape, making the Euphrates difficult to follow. It became harder to concentrate as the temperature increased and Amy, still **ensconced** in her flying suit, became a simmering pressure cooker jolted around the cockpit as *Jason* bounced through the **thermal eddies** that

---

ensconced settled in comfort
thermal eddies currents of air created by warm air rising. They cause turbulence

turned the sky into a badly surfaced road. She pushed him higher to escape the heat. But at 7000 feet the air was hazy and visibility poor. She had lost sight of the guiding river and wondered whether she would be able to see anything at all in the gloom that lay ahead. Peering at her map, she guessed she was flying through a section marked only as 'unsurveyed desert'. It was impossible to tell in which direction the sand was blowing; she tried to follow faint tracks below her but these inevitably faded into nothingness. Once she spotted a caravan of horses and camels but as soon as she tried to get close the animals and their riders scattered in panic.

Without any warning *Jason's* nose dipped, the propeller slowed momentarily and the plane plunged several thousand feet towards the ground. While Amy struggled to steady the machine and recover from the physical shock of being hurled through the air, the same thing happened again. *Jason* lurched towards the ground a total of three times, pausing momentarily on each occasion like a runaway elevator that allows its passengers to regain their heads and stomachs before subjecting them to the next jolt. She felt so disorientated that it was impossible to be sure that she was not flying upside down.

The final plunge left *Jason* a few feet above ground; dust and wind batted the plane from side to side. Amy's goggles were covered with sand and her eyes smarted with the effort of trying to make out what was happening to her. She felt *Jason's* wheels touch down at around 110 miles per hour and tried to steer into the wind in an effort to slow the machine, fearing that the plane would at any minute flip over or hit some obstacle. When *Jason* finally stopped Amy switched off the engine and struggled out of the cockpit. The howling wind, smarting sand and her bulky parachute made every movement a huge physical effort. She pulled the machine round so that it faced into the wind but the Gypsy Moth, built without brakes, was immediately blown backwards. Amy struggled onto the plane, now flapping about like a cornered bird, and dragged luggage from the front cockpit to put it behind the wheels.

Her priority was to protect *Jason*, her only means of escape from the desert. The dust stung her face as she battled from one side of the plane to the other, trying to cover the engine and protect the carburettor from the sand and dust. Just as she thought she had secured the canvas on one side the wind wrenched it away before she had fixed the opposite side. It took her thirty minutes to lash the cover down. Her next task was to climb onto the engine to tie her hanky over the air-vent hole in the petrol tank to try to keep the sand out.

Having made her plane as safe as possible, she sat with her back to the wind on *Jason's* tail in a bid to fix him to the ground. She could see barely a few feet in any direction; she had no idea where she was. 'I had never been so frightened in all my life', she said later. Her only option was to wait, a prisoner in the wind's **cacophony**, until the storm subsided. Once she heard the eerie sound of barking in the distance and, remembering the stories of the wild desert dogs who tore their prey apart, she retrieved her small pistol and sat with it at the ready.

After three hours the wind began to die down and the air cleared. Fearing that this might be her one chance of escape, Amy darted around *Jason*, uncovering the engine and hurling her luggage back into the front cockpit. In her panic, she dropped tools which were immediately covered by sand and lost for ever to the desert.

Jason's engine started at the first swing of the propeller and Amy pointed the engine in an easterly direction, hopeful that this would take her towards Baghdad. If her instinct was wrong she was heading

---

cacophony loud, unpleasant noise

deeper into the desert and towards a slow death from dehydration. This was an end that pilots feared more than any other; the crazed scribblings left by parched airmen revealed the slowest and most torturous of deaths. Amy imagined her bones being found 'many, long years' after her death; a grim flight of fancy that was itself wildly optimistic.

Although visibility was still difficult she soon spotted what she believed to be the river Tigris. She followed this south until it was joined by what she hoped was the river Diyala. This gave her a 'fix' and she saw the flat, palm-fringed sprawl of Baghdad and the Imperial Airways Aerodrome. On landing *Jason* sank down on one wing and Amy discovered that one of his undercarriage **struts** had snapped during her forced landing in the desert.

She set off to walk to the distant hangars but a lorry sped out to pick her up. Her relief at hearing English voices was immense. She peeled off her Sidcot suit and discussed what to do about *Jason*. At first it seemed she would have to wait for a replacement to be sent from the nearest De Havilland depot 1500 miles away at Karachi in western India (now Pakistan). Amy was devastated by this news which meant she had no chance of beating **Hinkler**. However, the presence of an RAF aerodrome at nearby Hinaidi provided some hope and the Imperial Airways manager suggested sending the strut to the RAF aerodrome, where ten engineers worked through the night to repair it.

---

strut bar forming part of framework that supported the body of the plane
Hinkler the first person to fly solo from England to Australia; Amy Johnson was trying to beat his record

Terra Incognita, Travels In Antarctica

by *Sara Wheeler*

In this book about her own travels to Antarctica, the writer tells the story of an earlier group of explorers. Her dramatic use of language and skilful drawing of characters enable the reader to share the horror and excitement of their journey. As you read this extract you should focus upon:

- the language the writer uses to convey the dangers and difficulties of the journey
- the attention the writer pays to the sounds of words and the rhythms of sentences
- attention the writer pays to the structure of the writing.

The writer relates the experiences of Ernest Shackleton's Imperial Trans-Antarctic Expedition, which left London in 1914. Shackleton's party planned to sledge across the Antarctic from the Weddell Sea, but their ship, Endurance, was caught in pack ice and sank. After rescuing two pounds (about a kilo) of belongings each, they drifted on ice floes and then travelled in the three lifeboats to Elephant Island.

They reached the island as winter was beginning and there was no hope of rescue. One of the men, James Worsley, worked out the distances to Georgia, the Falklands and Cape Horn and it was decided that six of the men should take one of the lifeboats, the James Caird, *to the whaling stations of South Georgia, 700 miles away.*

At ten o'clock on Easter Monday morning, 1916, a diminutive wooden boat lurched off a rock shelf on one of the islands to the north of the Antarctic Peninsula and into the angry Southern Ocean, immediately tossing two of the men on board into the broth. Within minutes the freezing waters of a roller were pouring through the plughole. Standing on the sandless and wind-whipped beach behind, a tall Anglo-Irishman was calmly making final preparations before himself climbing into the boat. His name was Ernest Shackleton.

The two sodden men were pushed ashore with an oar, the anchor was dropped, the hole was plugged with a filthy handkerchief until the real plug was found, stores and over a ton of ballast were stowed, and at half-past twelve Shackleton gave the order to set sail. For 137 days the twenty-two men left behind grew blubbery on seal and penguin underneath a pair of upturned boats, watching themselves grow old as the chance of rescue, slim at the outset, shrank to an almost imperceptible filament of hope. The story of their rescue is the greatest epic in the history of Antarctica.

Six of them went, and Worsley was at the helm. Before they left, Shackleton issued instructions to Frank Wild, the leader of the stranded party, to the effect that if relief had not arrived in six months, when the whaling station opened on Deception Island, Wild was to assume the boat had gone down and set out himself.

Worsley recorded in his diary that on the first evening, with the Southern Cross overhead, Shackleton sent the rest in to sleep and the two of them 'snuggled close together all night', relentlessly inundated by waves and 'holding north by the stars that swept in glittering procession over the Atlantic towards the Pacific ... While I steered, his arm thrown over my shoulder, we discussed plans and yarned in low tones. We smoked all night – he rolled cigarettes for us both, a job at which I was unhandy.' They had one compass, and it was faulty. Shackleton confided that if any of the twenty-two perished, he would feel like a murderer. Worsley's account of how he navigated by **dead reckoning** beggars belief. He concluded his story, 'I often recall with proud affection memories of those hours with a great soul.'

Tom Crean, a petty officer in the navy, was in charge of the 'kitchen'. He was obliged to light the primus stove while bent double and jam it between his and another man's legs to keep it steady. There was no room for anyone to sit upright and eat their hoosh, the standard Antarctic meal of a dehydrated meat protein mixture dissolved in hot water. It was usually followed by a sledging biscuit, some Streimer's Nutfood and a few sugarlumps. By the third day everything, with the exception of matches and sugar in watertight tins, was irredeemably soaked. The men's feet and legs, immersed almost constantly, were already frostbitten and swollen.

---

dead reckoning working out the boat's location by estimating its direction and the distance they had travelled

They had rations, water and oil for thirty days. Apart from that, they didn't have much, except methylated spirits for the stove, a tin of sea oil, six reindeer-hair sleeping bags, a small sack of spare clothes and one chronometer. There wasn't enough room for them all to lie down at once, so they took it in turns to crawl on their chests and stomachs over sharp stone ballast, Shackleton directing the in–out operation, into a hole seven feet long and five feet wide. Then they slid into saturated sleeping bags which after a week began to smell of sour bread. The air was bad in there, and stifling, and sometimes they woke suddenly with the feeling that they had been buried alive.

By the fifth day John Vincent, able seaman and a bully, was experiencing severe pain in his legs and feet. He lost his appetite for the fight after that. It was the psychological cramp that did for him, not the physical kind. He had worked on North Sea trawlers too, so he was no stranger to hardship.

By the seventh day their faces and hands were black with soot and blubber. They needed calories, so they drank the seal oil. Two of the sleeping bags were proclaimed beyond redemption and tossed overboard, lifted briefly against the blanched sky.

On the eighth day the ice on the boat grew so thick that they were obliged to take to the *James Caird* with an axe. It was agonisingly painful work. Their thighs were inflamed by the chafing of wet clothes, and their lower legs turned a spectral white, and numb. The **painter** snapped, the sea-anchor was swept away and the white light of fear flashed through six souls as the biggest wave they had ever encountered crashed over the little boat. But by the eleventh day Worsley calculated that they had crossed the halfway mark. Two of the men found tobacco leaves floating in the bilges and laboriously dried them and rolled

---

painter a rope used for tying a boat to the land

them into cigarettes with toilet paper. By the thirteenth day frostbite had skinned their hands so frequently that they were ringed like the inside of a tree-trunk. Then they discovered that the remaining water was **brackish**.

As sunlight leaked into the sky on the fifteenth day, someone spotted a skein of seaweed. The hours ticked by. If they had missed South Georgia, they were lost. Then, at half-past twelve, as in a vision, a turban of clouds unravelled on the pearly horizon and revealed a shining black crag. It was land. It was in fact Cape Demidov, the northern headline of King Haakon Sound on South Georgia. What they didn't know, as they celebrated, was that the worst was not behind them. It was still to come.

A gale got up. The wind and current were against them, forcing the *James Caird* almost onto the rocks. It began to snow, and roaring breakers shattered into the mist. It looked hopeless. They steered, pumped and bailed, lying to each other with encouraging phrases. Their mouths and tongues were so swollen from thirst that they could barely swallow. At one point they were driven so close to land that they had to crane their necks to look up at the top of the crag. Tension took them, then, beyond speech. Worsley said later that for three hours they looked death square in the eye, and he felt annoyed that nobody would ever know they had got so far.

The ordeal lasted for nine hours, and then they knew that they were going to live. The storm subsided. On the seventeenth day they sailed on to the entrance of King Haakon Bay and got in. It was dark by the time they spotted a cove. They carried the boat in and heaved themselves ashore, eyes fixed on the glint of freshwater pools. Shackleton wrote later that they flung down the **adze**, logbook and cooker. 'That was all, except our wet

---

brackish slightly salty
adze a tool similar to an axe

clothes, that we brought out of the Antarctic, which we had entered a year and a half before with well-found ship, full equipment and high hopes. That was all of **tangible** things; but in memories we were rich.'

---

tangible real, touchable

A Covered Wagon Girl

These extracts from a young American girl's diary in the 1800s give us a privileged insight into her thoughts and feelings. As you read these extracts you should focus upon:

- the writer's use of language to record and explore her feelings honestly
- the possibility that she was writing for a larger audience than just herself.

On March 20, 1849 fourteen-year-old Sallie Hester and her family began a long journey from Indiana to the California Territory. Some pioneers went to California in search of the gold that had been discovered there, but the Hester family travelled to find a warmer climate, which they hoped would benefit Sallie's mother's poor health. They journeyed 2000 miles along the Oregon–California Trail, crossing dangerous rivers and deserts and enduring many hardships.

May 21

Camped on the beautiful Blue River, 215 miles [346 kilometres] from St Joe, with plenty of wood and water and good grazing for our cattle. Our family all in good health. When we left St Joe my mother had to be lifted in and out of the wagons; now she walks a mile or two without stopping, and gets in and out of the wagons as spry as a young girl. She is perfectly well. We had two deaths in our train within

the past week of cholera – young men going West to
seek their fortunes. We buried them on the banks of
the Blue River, far from home and friends. This is a
beautiful spot. The Plains are covered with flowers.
We are in the Pawnee Nation, a dangerous and
hostile tribe. We are obliged to watch them closely
and double our guards at night. They never make
their appearance during the day, but skulk around at
night, steal cattle and do all the mischief they can.
When we camp at night, we form a corral with our
wagons and pitch our tents on the outside, and inside
of this corral we drive our cattle, with guards
stationed on the outside of tents. We have a cooking
stove made of sheet iron, a portable table, tin plates
and cups, cheap knives and forks (best ones packed
away), camp stools, etc. We sleep in our wagons on
feather beds; the men who drive for us [sleep] in the
tent. We live on bacon, ham, rice, dried fruits,
molasses, packed butter, bread, coffee, tea, and milk
as we have our own cows. Occasionally some of the
men kill an antelope and then we have a feast; and
sometimes we have fish on Sunday.

Humboldt River (Nevada), August 20
We are now 348 miles [560 kilometres] from the
mines. We expect to travel that distance in three
weeks and a half. Water and grass scarce.

---

slough swamp

St Mary's River, August 25
Still travelling down the Humboldt. Grass has been
scarce until today. Though the water is not fit to
drink – slough* water – we are obliged to use it, for
it's all we have.

September 4
Stopped and cut grass for the cattle and supplied
ourselves with water for the desert. Had a trying time
crossing. Several of our cattle gave out and we left
one. Our journey through the desert was from
Monday, three o'clock in the afternoon, until
Thursday morning at sunrise, September 6. The
weary journey last night, the mooing of the cattle for
water, their exhausted condition, with the cry of
'Another ox down,' the stopping of the train to
unyoke the poor dying brute, to let him follow at will
or stop by the wayside and die, and the weary, weary
tramp of men and beasts worn out with heat and
famished for water, will never be erased from my
memory. Just at dawn, in the distance, we had a
glimpse of the Truckee River, with it the feeling:
Saved at last! Poor cattle; they kept on mooing,
even when they stood knee deep in water. The long
dreaded desert had been crossed and we are all safe
and well. Here we rested Thursday and Friday –
grass green and beautiful, and the cattle are up to
their eyes in it.

Don't Let's Go to the Dogs Tonight

by *Alexandra Fuller*

In this extract the writer relates an exciting event in a way that gives a vibrant picture of her mother's heroism, courage and determination. As you read this extract you should focus upon:

- the way character is revealed through speech
- the way the writer describes hazards and obstacles to highlight her mother's courage
- the way character is revealed through actions.

The writer was the daughter of white settlers in Rhodesia (now Zimbabwe) in southern Africa. This book is a memoir of her life as a schoolgirl in a country undergoing civil war.

Alexandra's father is away fighting; the armed man who is supposed to protect the family is useless, regarded by Alexandra's mother as 'just one more kid to take care of' and their farm has been invaded by stray cattle that threaten to spread disease to their own dairy cattle. With no one to turn to for help, Alexandra's mother makes up her mind to round up all the stray cattle and hold a 'cow sale'.

That day Mum and I rode up into the foothills on game paths and tracks the terrorists have used. These paths are already strangled with fresh growth, with the promise of a new rainy season coming, the quick green threads of creepers stretching over old, dry tracks, swallowing footpaths, and demonstrating how quickly this part of Africa would reclaim its wild lands if it were left untrodden. The horses struggle over rocks, their unshod hooves slipping against the hard ground as we climb ever higher into the mountains. Mum rides ahead on her big bay thoroughbred, an ex-trotter rescued from an abusive home and made rideable again under Mum's patient training. I am on my fat chestnut pony, Burma Boy, a bad-tempered and ill-behaved animal; bucking, bolting, kicking, and biting regularly – all of which, Dad says, is good for me. The dogs swarm, noses down, through the bush ahead of us, yelping with excitement when they put up a hare or mongoose and bounding hysterically through the bush if they catch sight of a **duiker** or wild pig.

By late morning, we are on the border of our farm in the high, thick bush, as close to Mozambique as I have ever been on a horse.

'Keep your eyes peeled for buffalo bean,' says Mum.

I start to itch at once and look ahead nervously. Buffalo bean is a creeper boasting an attractive purple bloom in the spring, followed by a mass of beans that are covered in tiny velvet hairs, which blow off in the wind and can lodge in your skin. The hairs can stimulate a reaction so severe, so burning and persistent, that it has been known to send grown men mad, tearing into the bush in search of mud in which to roll to alleviate the torture. I am also compelled to crouch, my head pressed against Burma Boy's neck, to avoid the strong, elaborate webs that spread taut across our path. In the middle of these bright, tight webs there are bid red and yellow-legged spiders waiting hopefully for prey to fall. Burma Boy's ears are laced with the silvery threads.

Mum is following the native cattle trails, fresh manure and tracks and freshly disturbed bush; she pushes on and on, occasionally getting off her horse to inspect the ground and then riding on with more confidence.

duiker small antelope

'They've gone this way. See?' The cows have stayed close to the springs that feed out of the mountains and run through these foothills to come down into the rivers in the heart of our farm.

'Look,' says Mum fiercely, 'bloody cows! Look!' She points at the damaged stream banks and kicks Caesar on with fresh determination, her face set in a scowl. The horses are straining, wet with sweat and frothing white under the tail and mane. Even the dogs have stopped following their noses and bounding ahead after wild game scents; they are beginning to follow closely on the horses' heels, tongues lolling. I say, 'Are we nearly there yet?' I am starting to get thirsty and we have brought nothing with us to drink.

Mum says, 'Stop whinging.'

'I'm not whinging. I was just *saying*.'

'Start looking for mombies.'

The cattle that have stayed up this high are wild. As quickly as we cover their fresh tracks, they move on, staying ahead of us, out of sight and almost beyond earshot. Mum says, 'I'm going to go around. You stay here, and catch them if they come down.' She pushes Caesar into the thick bush with the dogs scrambling behind her, and soon disappears from sight. For a while I can hear her and the dogs as they make their way through the bush, and then there is silence. I hold my breath and listen. I am surrounded by the high, whining noise of insects – their frantic spring singing in the dry grass – and by the occasional shriek of an invisible bird. Burma Boy puts his head down and starts to pull at the thin, bitter dry grass. It is very hot and still and I am enveloped in the salty steam sent up by Burma Boy as he sweats; my fingers sting against the leather reins and my eyes burn. Sweat drips down from my hatband and flies swarm onto our stillness to take advantage of the moisture, crawling over my eyes and lips until I swat them away. I am very thirsty now.

'Mu-um.' My voice sounds high and thin in the heat.

I wait. There is no answer. I hold my breath and then call again, louder, 'Mu-uum!' Still no answer. I look around, suddenly imagining that terrorists might crawl up on me at any moment and take me by surprise. I wonder where Mum has gone; she has the gun with her. I wonder if she will hear me if I am attacked by terrorists. I close my eyes and take a deep breath. What will Burma Boy do if we are suddenly surrounded by terrorists? Bolt, no doubt. And I will be scraped off on a tree and lie winded and wounded on the ground waiting for Mum to come and rescue me. I wonder how she would find me again in this thick bush. I'd be dead by then. Eyelids chopped off and fried, no ears, no lips. Dead. Burma Boy would be home. They would have a funeral for me, like the funeral we had for Olivia. They would say how brave I was. I start to cry. I would be buried, next to my fried eyelids, lips and ears, in a little coffin. There would be a hump of fresh earth, crawling with earthworms, piled over me in the little settlers' cemetery. Tears stream down my face. The *Umtali Post* will write a moving article about my death.

'Mum!' I shout, genuinely frightened.

Burma Boy throws up his head at my alarm.

'It's okay,' I say shakily, crying and running my hand down his wet neck. 'It's okay.'

I start to imagine that Mum, Caesar, and the dogs have been caught by terrorists themselves. Maybe Mum is lying in a bloody puddle, eyelidless and lipless, with the dogs licking helplessly, lovingly at her lifeless hands. I will be brave at Mum's funeral. The *Umtali Post* will write an article about me, lost and alone in the bush, while my mother lay dead surrounded by her faithful dogs and loyal horse. I turn Burma Boy around. 'Do you know the way home?' I ask, letting him have his head. But he, after looking around for a few moments, placidly puts his head down and starts to eat again.

It feels like a long time during which I alternated between quiet, dry panic and noisy, copious weeping before I hear Mum and the dogs coming through the bush. Mum is singing, like the herdsmen taking the cows to the dip, 'Here dip-dip-dip-dip dip! Dip, dip-dip-dip-dip dip!' And in front of her there are a dozen multicoloured cows, running with heads held high, wild and frightened, their eyes white-rimmed, their long, unruly horns slashing at the bush. Burma Boy throws up his head, startled, and shies. I pull up the reins. Mum says, 'Get behind me.'

I start to cry with relief at seeing her. 'I thought you were lost.'

'Out the way,' she shouts, 'out the way! Get behind!'

I pull Burma Boy around.

'Come on,' says Mum, riding past me, 'let's herd this lot down.'

I say, 'You were so long.'

'Catch the cows as they come through.'

But the cows are not used to being herded and are unwilling and frightened participants. They break loose frequently and Mum has to circle back to bring the herd into order. She has identified the leader, a tall-hipped ox with a very old, almost worn-through leather strap around his neck that once must have held a bell. All the cows are dripping with ticks: their ears are crusted with small red ticks and their bodies are bumped with the raised grey engorged adults, which look ready to drop off. Mum says, 'If we can keep the leader going, the rest might follow.' But it still takes us more than an hour to move the cows less than half a mile. I start to cry again.

'What's the matter now?' says Mum irritably.

'I'm thirsty,' I cry, 'I'm tired.'

'Well, you go on home, then,' says Mum. 'I'm bringing these cows down.'

'But I don't know the way.'

'Fergodsake,' says Mum between her teeth.

I start to cry even harder.

She says, 'Give Burma Boy his head, he'll take you home.'

But Burma Boy, given his head, is content to follow Caesar and graze happily at this leisurely pace. 'Look, he won't go home.'

'Then *ride* him.'

I kick feebly, 'I'm thirsty,' I whine.

Mum is unrelenting. 'So let's get these cows home. The sooner we get these cows home the sooner you'll have something to drink.'

We ride on for two more hours. I slouch over my saddle, letting myself rock lazily with Burma Boy's tread. I make no attempt to herd the cows.

Mum scowls at me with irritation: *'Ride* your bloody horse.'

I flap my legs and pull weakly at the reins. 'He won't listen.'

'Don't be so bloody feeble.'

Fresh tears spring into my eyes. 'I'm not being feeble.'

Mum says, 'If you would help, we'd get home a lot sooner.'

We ride on in hostile silence for another half an hour or so. Then I say, 'I think I have buffalo bean.' I start to scratch fretfully. I am so thirsty that my tongue feels dry and cracking. 'I'm going to faint, I'm so thirsty.'

Mum circles back to catch a stray cow.

'Mu-uuum.'

She isn't going to listen. It is no good. It is clear that I am not going to get home until the cows are safely fenced up in the home paddocks. I pull Burma Boy's head up and circle him back to the lagging cows, straggling at the rear of the herd. 'Dip, dip-dip-dip-dip dip,' I sing, my voice dry on the hot air. 'Dip, dip-dip-dip-dip-dip-dip.'

One of the cows tries to run out of the herd and break for the bush. I dig my heels into Burma Boy's sides and spin him around, catching the cow before she can escape.

'That's it,' says Mum, 'that's better. Keep it up.'

It takes until late afternoon to get the cows down to the home paddocks, by which time the cows' flanks are wet with sweat, their horn-heavy heads are low and swinging; they are tripping forward without thought of a fight. I have stopped snivelling, but am hunched over the front of my saddle trying not to think about how thirsty I am.

'There,' says Mum, wiping the sweat off her top lip as she shuts the gate behind the wild cows, 'that's not a bad day's work.'

I shrug miserably.

'Don't you think?'

'I s'pose.'

Mum swings up on Caesar and pats him on the rump. 'You know, we're descended from cattle rustlers, you and me,' she tells me, her eyes shining. 'In Scotland, our family were cattle rustlers.'

I think, *At least Scotland is cool. At least there are streams of fresh water to drink from. At least Scottish cows don't lead you into buffalo bean.*

* * *

The next day Mum sends the cattle boys into the nearby villages. She says, 'Tell the villagers I have their cows. If they want their cows back, they can come and get them.' She pauses. 'But they'll have to pay me for grazing,' she says slowly. 'Understand? Lots and lots of money for grazing and for taking care of their cows. Hey? *Mazvinzwa*? Do you understand?'

'Eh-eh, madam.'

No one comes to collect their cows. Mum dips the cows, deworms them, brands them with our brand, feeds them up on the Rhodes grass until their skins are shiny and they are so fat it seems as if they might burst, and then sends them on the red lorry into Umtali, to the Cold Storage Corporation, to be sold as ration meat. With the proceeds, she buys a plane ticket for Vanessa to visit Granny and Grandbra in England and she pays for the rest of us to drive down to South Africa on a camping holiday where we are flooded out of our tent on the second night on the West Coast and subsequently spend a damp, drunken fortnight in a grey fishing village trying to avoid hostile Afrikaners and waiting for the sun to come out.

That is the year I turn ten. The year before the war ends.

Activities

In Black and White

1 This extract is imaginatively crafted to build up tension in a variety of ways. Explore how the writer does this by collecting ideas in a table like the one below. Leave space in your table to add two or three more points of your own.

Point	Example	Explanation
Precise times are mentioned in the build-up to the start of the race.	4.55 and 4.58	At times of high tension, time often seems to pass very slowly, allowing events to be recalled in minute detail.
The first paragraph uses dramatic language to show the significance of the race.	The race is seen as *the most prestigious event of the entire Olympiad* and the *defining moment of his life.*	The use of the words *most* and *entire* lend *emphasis* and *defining moment* suggests that Owens knows that this performance is the one for which he will be remembered.
In the first paragraph it is made clear that Owens was competing not only for his own country but also as a representative against the Nazis' racism.	Owens is called a *Negro* and Borchmeyer was seen by Hitler to be *competing for Nazi Germany.*	
Metcalfe is portrayed as a man who is determined to win the race and as a threat to Owens.		
The great length of the training undergone by Owens is compared with the brief nature of the race.		
As the race starts, McRae writes in very short paragraphs.		

2 Having added your own points, supported by examples and explanations, use all the information in the table to write an answer to the question: How is tension created in this passage?

3 Show your own ability to build up tension and excitement by imagining that you are a sports commentator working for the BBC and writing your commentary on the race from the time just before the runners' names are announced. Remember that the race itself only lasts just over 10 seconds (although you can spend longer on the events just before and just after the race) and that most of your commentary should be in the present tense. At the most dramatic points of the race you will probably want to use short sentences or fragments of sentences and exclamations, while your comments before and after the race will be more developed.

The Cruellest Miles

1 Part of the writers' craft in this passage is to explain the dangers faced by the dog sled team so that the reader can share in the drama of the story. What do we learn of the dangers and difficulties of the expedition?

   a What was the first difficulty that Shannon encountered on his journey?

   b Explain the dangers presented by river ice, overflow and drum ice.

   c Explain the danger to Shannon of letting his body become too cold.

   d How do teams of dogs behave when they become too tired?

2 Shannon is the human hero in this event and like heroes from fiction he has to make the right decisions. Highlighting the decisions he has to make helps to build both character and tension.

a Make a list of the decisions that Shannon had to make on his journey to Campbell's roadhouse.

b In making each of these decisions, what qualities did Shannon reveal?

3 Blackie is the animal hero of the event. Like animal heroes from fiction, he has particular skills to which the writers draw attention. Find **three** pieces of evidence from the text that suggest that Blackie was a good leading dog for the team.

4 The writers use a variety of techniques to involve the reader in the excitement of the event.

a The writers have very deliberately concentrated on the action of the event. They give very little description but what they do give helps to heighten the tension. Use the bullet points below to explore how.

- pick out the one, short paragraph that describes place
- explain what feelings this description creates in the reader
- say why the description is so short.

b On several other occasions the writers use paragraphs consisting of no more than two sentences. Find these paragraphs, identify what they have in common and say why they are effective.

c At the end of the extract it is clear that the writers want the reader to understand just how dangerous the journey had been for both man and dogs. This understanding of the danger adds to the drama but the writers do not attempt to over-dramatise the situation.

- What is the effect in the final paragraph of using short sentences and simple language?
- The use of numbers often tells us that we are dealing with bare facts. Where do we find these bare facts in the final paragraph? What is their effect?

5 Think of a time when someone you know or have heard of, was racing against time to do something important. Recreate the drama of the event in a piece of narrative writing. You should:

- set out the difficulties faced by the central character
- show that character's heroism by making clear the decisions s/he had to make
- use only very limited description
- use short sentences and paragraphs
- make your language powerful and direct.

Set your writing out in the middle of the page, leaving a wide border all around it. When you have completed your writing, annotate it to draw attention to the parts that best illustrate the bullet points above.

Amy Johnson, Queen of the Air

1 The writer makes this extract dramatic by selecting the events to show the reader the swift changes between good fortune and near disaster. Chart these changes in fortune on a line graph. On the horizontal axis you should have the events of the day and on the vertical axis you should have very bad luck at the bottom and very good luck at the top, with other points labelled in between.

2 Part of the impact of this event derives from Amy Johnson's inability to be certain where she was or where she was heading, and this uncertainty is shared by the reader. Look carefully at the section from, *But at 7000 feet* … to the end of the first paragraph. Pick out the words and phrases that convey that sense of uncertainty or lack of clarity, e.g. *air was hazy*, *gloom*, *peering*. What is the effect of piling these all up together?

3 Similes and metaphors are features of literary writing. In this passage the writer uses them to make Amy Johnson's experiences and feelings vivid for the reader. Choose **two** of the sentences below from the extract, explain what they mean and comment on the effect of the simile or metaphor (underlined) in each.

- *It became harder to concentrate as the temperature increased and Amy, still ensconced in her flying suit, <u>became a simmering pressure cooker</u> jolted around the cockpit as Jason bounced through the thermal eddies <u>that turned the sky into a badly surfaced road</u>.*
- *Jason lurched towards the ground a total of three times, pausing momentarily on each occasion <u>like a runaway elevator that allows its passengers to regain their heads and stomachs before subjecting them to the next jolt</u>.*
- *Amy struggled onto the plane, <u>now flapping about like a cornered bird</u>, and dragged luggage from the front cockpit to put it behind the wheels.*
- *Her only option was to wait, <u>a prisoner in the wind's cacophony,</u> until the storm subsided.*

4 Everything happens at great speed and the writer uses powerful verbs to express this. Find four examples of these verbs and comment on why each one is effective.

5 Show your understanding of how the writer conveys the drama of this event and write a short critical essay in answer to the question: How does the writer make this event dramatic? Write four paragraphs, drawing on your responses to questions 1–4 above. Quote from the text to support the points you make. Consider:

- the nature of the events themselves
- the uncertainty of the situation described
- the use of similes and metaphors
- the use of vivid language.

Terra Incognita, Travels in Antarctica

1 The writer makes her opening dramatic. Find quotations from the first paragraph where the writer:

- pinpoints the exact time the boat sets sail to show how momentous an occasion this was for the men
- uses adjectives to describe the boat, drawing attention to how unsuited it was for the journey
- uses powerful language to describe the dangers of the sea, especially when contrasted with the fragility of the boat
- draws attention to the fact that Shackleton did not appear frightened when he was standing on the beach; he is portrayed as the composed hero on the brink of adventure
- leaves the naming of the hero until the very end of the paragraph and then gives his name in a short, simple sentence. This heightens the dramatic effect, especially as this is a name many readers will recognise.

2 The writer uses emotive, descriptive language and the shape and rhythm of sentences to produce responses in the reader. Consider the examples in **a** and **b** below.

a *The painter snapped, the sea-anchor was swept away and the white light of fear flashed through six souls as the biggest wave they had ever encountered crashed over the little boat.*

- What is the effect of having the triplet of consequences of the crashing wave at the beginning of the sentence?
- What is the effect of using the adjectives *biggest* and *little* to describe the wave and the boat?
- Explain the effect of the verb *crashed*.

b *Then, at half-past twelve, as in a vision, the turban of clouds unravelled on the pearly horizon and revealed a shining black crag.*

- What is the effect of saving *revealed a shining black crag* until the end of the sentence?
- In what kind of writing would you expect to find the words *as in a vision*. What is the effect of using them here?
- How do the words *pearly* and *shining* make the reader feel?

3 Part of the writer's craft in making the writing dramatic is to convey to the reader the tremendous difficulties the men had to overcome. Make a list of the hardships faced by the men in the lifeboat and put them in order according to which *you* would find most difficult to bear. Put the most difficult at the top and the least difficult at the bottom. Write a sentence to justify your first and last choices.

4 In this extract, the writer presents the reader with a hero to admire. Choose **three** quotations from the extract that you think best reveal the character of Shackleton. What does each of your quotations show about his character?

5 The structure of a piece of writing is very important. Look at the middle section of the writing. Each of these paragraphs begins in one of two ways. Identify the two different ways in which they start and then explain how this helps to structure the writing.

6 With a partner, look carefully at the final three paragraphs of the extract. List everything of interest about the way they are written. Use bullet points and note form, for example:

- *As sunlight leaked* – makes the sunlight seem weak or feeble – contrasts with the more usual idea of sunlight *flooding*
- *The hours ticked by* – very short sentence – emphasises how long they had to wait

A Covered Wagon Girl

1 In this extract the writer gives an honest account of her feelings. As she was writing a diary we might suppose that she was writing entirely for herself, to document and explore her experiences. Explore how her language choices reflect her need to express herself in writing.

a It is clear that travelling was not easy.

- How many times does the writer use the word *weary*?
- Why do you think she uses this word more that any other to suggest that the journey was tiring?
- What other words does she use to suggest the same idea?

b Look at the diary entry for the day you think was best for Sallie.

- Which words make you think that this was the best day?
- Suggest a word of your own to sum up Sallie's feelings on that day.

c Once in this extract Sallie says that she has seen something that she will never forget. Find this and explain why it was unforgettable.

d Look at the way Sallie describes the Pawnee Nation in her entry for 21 May.

- What adjectives does she choose to describe these people?
- Which verb does she choose to describe their movements at night? What is the effect of that choice of verb?

2 For most of the time, Sallie does not write in complete sentences. Why is this kind of writing appropriate here?

3 This is a diary and, as such, we would expect it to be private. However, is there anything that suggests that this was written partly as a historical record? Look for information that appears to be informing other people about how Sallie and her family lived and travelled.

4 Think of a time when you have been moving on. Perhaps you have moved home, moved from one school to another or even from one country to another. Think back to that time and recreate the diary you might have written. Express your feelings as honestly and clearly as you can. Think about whether this would have been a piece of writing for your own eyes only or whether you could share it with others as a historical document.

Don't Let's Go to the Dogs Tonight

1 In order to highlight her mother's courage, the writer chooses to tell the reader about all the problems facing her mother. The farm is seen as a place full of difficulties and dangers. List all the problems presented by the African countryside under the headings **Terrain** (what the ground is like), **Fauna** (the animals), **Flora** (the plants), and say what dangers or problems they present.

2 A skilful writer does not always need to describe a character. At no time in the extract does the writer describe her mother, yet we get a clear picture of her personality by being told about what she says and does.

a Find three examples of things that Mum says. Make a table like the one below; beside each piece of direct speech write a word or two, saying what it tells the reader about Mum's character. Then write a sentence or two beside each quotation to explain your thinking.

Quotation	Mum's character	Explanation
Stop whinging	Impatient and unsympathetic	Mum's response to Alexandra's asking for a drink is curt and could be regarded as snappy. She allows nothing to stand in the way of the task she has to do.

b Find **three** examples of things that Mum does. You could write these as quotations or you could paraphrase (write them in your own words). Say what each one tells the reader about her character and comment on how the writer's use of language helps to convey this impression.

Action	Mum's character	Comment
Mum dips the cows, deworms them, brands them with our brand, feeds them on the Rhodes grass until their skins are shiny and they are so fat it seems as if they might burst, and then sends them on the red lorry into Umtali to the Cold Storage Corporation, to be sold as ration meat.	Capable, efficient	Mum's actions are given as a list divided by commas, which suggests that she does a lot of different things quickly and in a definite order to achieve the final outcome.

3 Look at all your responses above. We know that Mum was able to overcome the difficulties presented by the landscape; we also know a good deal about her personality. Now, write three paragraphs about why we admire Alexandra Fuller's mother. Be sure to include well-integrated, short quotations from the text.

4 Think of a person you admire. Do not describe that person, but instead think of an event that reveals their qualities. Tell that story in between 150 and 250 words, remembering to include some properly punctuated direct speech.

Comparing the extracts

The extracts in this section are all about drama and tension.
The following activities ask you to draw some comparisons
between the texts in terms of:

- the purpose of the writing
- the audience for the writing
- the way the writing is crafted according to purpose and
  audience
- the impact the writing has on you as a reader.

The final activity asks you to make some judgements about
each of the extracts in this section and come to some
conclusions about whether they are *literary* non-fiction.

1 You and a partner have been asked to compile a list for a
   magazine feature called 'One Hundred Brave Men and
   Women'.

   - Which of the people featured in this section would you
     include in your list? Give reasons.
   - The list is to be arranged in order, starting with the
     bravest. Where would you put the people you have
     chosen?
   - Which other brave people would you want to include in
     the list? Where would you put them?
   - Your editor has asked you to write about 100 words
     about each person on the list, saying why they have
     been selected. Choose **one** person that you have read
     about in this section and then write a draft. Suggest a
     picture to go with the entry.

2 *The Cruellest Miles* is set in the Arctic and *Terra Incognita*
   in the Antarctic. Both tell of people desperate to reach the
   ends of their journey because lives are at stake.

Both make the reader share the drama of the situation.
Copy and complete the table below to show how the
writers create tension. Make extra rows to add suggestions
of your own.

Feature	Example from *The Cruellest Miles*	Comments	Example from *Terra Incognita*	Comments and comparison
Vivid description of the hazards presented by the landscape				
Use of powerful vocabulary to suggest danger				
Use of short dramatic sentences				
Writer's comments showing the courage of the central character				
Implications that the central character is not saying how frightening the situation is				
Factual information revealing danger				

3 Think about any race that you have watched or taken part
  in. Write about it in as exciting a way as you can, using
  some of the techniques employed by the writers in this
  section.

4 Choose the extract from this section that interested you
  most. Plan and write an article about the events for a local
  newspaper. Your report should show the pride the
  community feels in the courage shown by this local hero.
  Copy and fill in the planning grid below to help you.

Features	Your notes
An eye-catching headline (with alliteration and/or pun)	
Paragraph 1: main points of story – Who? What? Where? When? How? Why?	
Paragraph 2: an example of an event showing particular bravery	
Paragraph 3: another event showing courage	
Paragraph 4: a comment or quotation from the person involved and /or from a local supporter	
Paragraph 5: a comment summing up the feelings of the local community	

5 In working through these extracts you have explored a range of features that make them interesting or distinctive. All of them are about things that have really happened, so they are non-fiction rather than fiction. The crucial question is, are they *literary* non-fiction?

In small groups, working on a copy of the grid on page 199, review each of the texts and decide which of the criteria for literary non-fiction each one meets. Then decide which extracts are definitely literary non-fiction and which ones you are less confident about. Be prepared to share your judgements. Remember that there are no right and wrong answers!

Section 3

Observation: involvement in a writer's thoughts and memories

This section looks at literary non-fiction by writers who have drawn on their childhood experiences or events they have observed. They have presented them in ways that entertain and tell us something about the time they were written. While reading the extracts, it may be helpful to keep the following questions in mind.

- How do the writers use language in lively and imaginative ways to convey a sense of place or an event?
- What choices do the writers make when writing about past events?
- How can literary non-fiction use some of the patterns and structures of fiction?
- How can a range of different text types, such as letters or interviews, be used to create a sense of the past?

Extracts in this section

1 'Christmas at school' by William Woodruff
2 *My East End* by Gilda O'Neill
3 'Profiting from Child's Play' by George Rosie
4 'The Billycart Era' by Clive James
5 Letter from Randolph Caldecott, March 1873
6 Letter from Jane Austen to her sister

Why the extracts have been selected

Extracts 1–3 are all concerned with how children spend their time. Extracts 1 and 2 are autobiographical accounts where information may have been deliberately left out.

Extract 3 is an article in which the writer presents strong opinions. He uses his experiences to inform his opinions.

Extract 4 is included here because the writer has recreated a particular sense of time and place, deliberately drawing on the conventions of fiction, crafting and shaping his account like a short story.

Extracts 5–6 are letters in which the writers have been keen observers and want to pass their on observations in entertaining ways. They both employ techniques that make their accounts seem much more than just factual.

Christmas at school
by *William Woodruff*

In this extract from his autobiography, the writer uses highly descriptive language to recreate the atmosphere of his primary school. As you read this extract you should focus upon:
- the way the writer uses detail to build effective description
- the way he reveals his own feelings and sense of excitement.

The writer's memories of primary school go back almost a hundred years. For much of the time school was fairly dull, but in the weeks running up to Christmas it underwent a transformation and became a place filled with excited anticipation and frantic activity.

As Christmas approached, the school was transformed into a magic castle. A feeling of festivity filled the air. I must have been impressionable for I watched transfixed while teachers and students converted dark, crowded classrooms into glittering caves. Fluttering coloured paper streamers, pom-poms, Chinese lanterns, and decorations were hung from walls and ceilings. In the ever-present draughts, the great silver bells swung leisurely above our heads. When the gas lamps were lit in the afternoon, the magic grew.

The closer we got to Christmas, the more things changed. There was no thrashing. The cruel use of the Dunce's hat – which I feared more than anything – was temporarily suspended. Even Mr Manners and Joe took a rest from fighting. We didn't do a stitch of work. We played leap frog and had snowball fights in the school yard. We formed choirs and produced plays. For the plays we created scenery, properties and costumes out of nothing. It was great fun. I also learned something about language and **elocution**.

In one of the plays I was chosen to tip-toe into an artist's studio and place my head in the hole another student had made in the artist's canvas. The whole idea was that the artist would fail to notice that his canvas had been damaged and would go on touching up the face – my face – with paint. All I had to do was to put my head into the hole and keep absolutely still.

When the great night came, with most of our parents in attendance, I crept into the artist's studio. Having made sure that the artist was not there, I placed my head into the hole in the canvas. At that point the artist returned with his paints. This was the part we hadn't rehearsed. Instead of applying a dab of paint – as he had been instructed – he began to plaster me with the stuff. Howls of laughter came from the audience. When I opened my mouth to protest, he popped the paint brush right down my throat. By now the audience was uncomfortable. The play was considered a great success, but the taste of paint stayed with me for days.

Just before Christmas, the older boys carried in a Christmas tree dusted with snow. It was so high and so wide that they had difficulty getting it through the doors. I was thrilled when they hung the tree with decorations and candles. It became a mass of colour and light. I had never seen such a beautiful thing. How it contrasted with the dark day! They also brought in the crib with statues of Mary and Joseph, and the Infant Jesus, and the Three Wise Men from the East. There was a cow eating from the manger. These things brought home to me the joy and peace of Christmas for the first time.

---

elocution speaking clearly and well

While we were singing carols around the tree, a horse-drawn cart arrived laden with wooden crates filled with boxes of chocolates. The news spread like wildfire. Some kind soul had donated a box for every child. We shrieked with delight as box after box was **extricated** from the wood shavings. Each chocolate box lid was a delight in itself. My box showed a boy and a girl skating down a frozen river with snow-covered cottages lining the banks. It was sheer magic for me to possess such a prize. I kept the lid for ages.

At this time, my brother and sisters took me round the darkened streets singing carols. I carried a Chinese paper lantern with a candle inside. 'Christmas is coming,' we all chanted, 'the goose is getting fat, please put a penny in the old man's hat. If you haven't got a penny, a ha'penny will do. If you haven't got a ha'penny – God bless you.' We gave a lot of blessings and received some ha'pennies.

---

extricated taken out

My East End
by *Gilda O'Neill*

In this extract the writer draws together her own memories with those of people she has interviewed, to document a way of life that has disappeared. As you read this extract you should focus upon:
- the way the writer uses spoken language to make the account fresh and lively
- the way she uses detail to recreate a clear sense of place.

The writer was born and grew up in Bethnal Green, in the East End of London. She has collected stories and memories from hundreds of East Enders, giving a lively sense of what life was like in the area. This part of London has always been associated with poverty, but the writer shows that although there may have been little money, this simply encouraged children to make the best use of whatever was available to them.

We'd be out from first thing till it got pitch dark.

Children in east London spent much of their spare time outside amusing themselves: raking the streets and playing games with their friends, making do with a few toys and little purpose-built equipment, using, instead, their imagination and surprising inventiveness to create things to entertain them. It is amazing the uses to which old wheels can be put – everything, apparently, from making hoops and carts to constructing canal-dragging equipment.

As can be seen in these stories and memories of childhood, the phrase 'we made our own fun in them days' is a cliché which actually reflects the truth.

We made our own games then. Didn't cost nothing. Fashion a cricket bat out of something or other and play cricket in the middle of the road, using a manhole cover for a wicket. The only thing you had to watch was the windows, cos the streets were very narrow. Or we'd draw three lines across the street and make that a tennis court. We had an old ball and used our hands for bats. The game I really enjoyed - there were so many it's hard to choose - was called Release. There were probably about a dozen of you split into two teams. You'd spin up or whatever [toss a coin to decide] and six would run and the other six would try and catch them. You'd mark out a space on the pavement to use as a goal. If you were caught you'd get put there; stand there until everyone was caught on your side, then you'd change over and chase them. That used to be good, because if you used your loaf you could hang about round corners and dodge them. You'd wait till they had about four of your mates imprisoned on the pavement, then while they were distracted, looking for you, you'd run across the pavement goal and shout, 'Release!' And the ones who'd been captured would run off in all directions, all over the place. You'd run miles. Tire yourself out. It was great.

Mostly we just played out. Marbles in the gutter, hopscotch on the pavement, football on the road.

We had group games like cricket, with a home-made

---

cliché an over-used phrase

bat and three sticks for a wicket. These were physical,
rough and tumble games which sometimes resulted in a
severe reprimand when you got home. There was not a lot
of money for new clothes and we were threatened with not
being allowed out because we would have nothing left
to wear.

The toy I played with most was a hoop, which was a
bicycle-wheel rim with all the spokes taken out. I would
get a stick which fitted the hoop and just run all over
the place.

My childhood was happy. We were not surrounded by a
lot of children with wonderful toys making us envious
[and] there were no big stores filled with unobtainable
goodies. The only shop we knew with anything like
wonderful things was Woolworths. [Instead] we made our
own amusement. We had marbles, some clay and others
more valuable, called glarnies, made of glass, which we put
a value on depending on size. One enterprising invention
with marbles was [to] get a shoebox and cut small, arched
holes along one edge that would allow a marble to pass
through; mark a series of numbers over each one, up to ten,
then put the box upside down on the pavement. [The
object] was to get your marbles through the arches, from
several feet away. Those that didn't get through were taken
by the owner of the box. The size of the arch with ten above
it was just about legal. We also used to gamble with
cigarette cards. Each lad would have four or five, and you
would flick them in turn along the ground towards the
wall. When finished flicking, the nearest to the wall took
the lot.

Games had rules and a vocabulary, and there were rhymes to pronounce you 'out': ... 'One potato, two potato, three potato, four'. And crossed fingers and 'fainlights' gave you protection.

When I asked the respondents about whether they really were more naïve during their own childhoods than youngsters would appear to be today, the general view was that although people lived on top of one another, children were apart from the adults, leading almost separate lives, with their own childish and childlike concerns. It wasn't only that children were expected to be 'seen and not heard' but that grown-ups had little to do with, and often knew even less about, the carryings-on of the kids during both their school and their leisure time. It was this partial segregation that resulted in children being able to avoid more mature matters and sophisticated issues for far longer than those who are now exposed to an almost constant diet of adult concerns, worries and behaviours through the mass electronic and print media. Television, as will be seen in later chapters, was often cited as being a major source of change for the worse in all kinds of situations.

Profiting from Child's Play
by *George Rosie*

This extract differs from others in the section, in that it its purpose is to present opinions and convince the reader of a particular point of view. It achieves this not by using facts, but by giving a powerful personal and sometimes emotional perspective on how children's lives have changed. As you read this article you should focus upon:
- the way the writer uses powerful language to show the strength of his feelings
- the way the writer structures the article so that it moves from discussion of his own experience to wider issues
- how you respond to the points he makes.

The writer argues that the current generation of children have lost the ability to entertain themselves and make their own amusements. He thinks that children have been robbed of their natural instincts for play and fun by big business, which now dictates how we should spend our money and time. As you read, remember he is talking about you and your younger brothers and sisters. Do you think he is right, and if he is, does it matter?

Earlier this year I found myself in the Kunsthistorisches Museum in Vienna standing in front of a painting by Pieter Bruegel the Elder. I don't suppose it is one of the world's great paintings, or even one of Bruegel's best, but it is an exuberant, cheerful and life-enhancing piece of work. Done around 1560 and called *Kinderspiele* (Children's Games), it depicts the kind of thing that 16th-century Flemish kids got up to in their streets and playgrounds. And what these strangely garbed, long-dead

youngsters got up to was the same games that my generation used to play in the streets of north Edinburgh in the 1940s and 1950s.

It was quite startling. All our old Granton and Newhaven favourites are there, in Bruegel's picture. The game we called 'cuddy gi'e wey' where we piled on one another's backs until the whole structure collapsed in one shouting, laughing tangle; 'girds and cleeks' (more widely known as 'hoops and sticks'); 'collie-back fights' (unhorsing one boy from the back of another); whips and 'peeries'; skipping ropes, running across two rows of outstretched legs; leap frog; dressing up (a favourite with the girls); blindman's buff.

In Bruegel's painting there are **bairns** climbing trees, standing on their hands, playing horses on fences and chasing one another around for no particular reason. You

bairns children

can almost hear the shrieks and screams. *Kinderspiele* is a scene of that amiable, well-constructed chaos that only energetic children can generate. Take away the late medieval clothes (and the trees) and it could have been set in Newhaven's Primary School circa 1950.

But the longer I stared at the painting the sadder I became. That day in Vienna I began to sense a genuine tragedy. Because I could not remember the last time I saw a child in Scotland (or anywhere else in Britain) playing any of these games that were so familiar to Pieter Bruegel and to me. There may have been more than 400 years between his generation and mine, but the games we played were the same. No more. In one generation the rich, vigorous and probably ancient children's culture of north Europe seems to have disappeared, almost certainly for ever.

Which begs the question, why? What has happened? Why are our children and grandchildren so unfamiliar with all these venerable games and pastimes? I suppose the answers are obvious; the advent of the motor car which made the streets unsafe to play in; the advent of the television which preoccupied them while they were safely indoors; and the moral panics about murderers and paedophiles which have convinced so many parents that outdoors – anywhere outdoors – is fraught with danger.

Roaming the streets of Granton on clear frosty nights was one of the great pleasures of my childhood. There were decisions to be made, sides to be picked, complex games to be organised. Many of them seemed better after dark. They had names like 'kick the can', 'levey', and one we called 'white horse' for reasons that I could never fathom. We played until we were passing out with exhaustion or our mothers hauled us in for tea and/or neglected homework.

This is not – or at least not just – **nostalgia**. There was a powerful, absorbing street culture at work. It was very

---

nostalgia thinking of earlier times as being better than they really were real. And it belonged to us. Adults had no part in it. They only appeared if things got out of hand (too much noise in a stair, for example). Otherwise we were left to our own devices, which were very considerable. Which meant that when we turned loose on the streets, we had *something* to do. The kind of dismal, child-perpetrated vandalism that is now common was very rare. We knew – quite literally – how to amuse ourselves.

But what kid under 10 nowadays knows how to organise a game of levey? Or how to play 'high setoosh, low setoosh' with a ball against a wall? Or chalk out a **peever bed**? Very few, I suspect. Pieter Bruegel's children did. The children of the 1940s and 1950s certainly did. But our children do not. Their own culture is gone. It has been replaced by an **inane** variety of pop music, television and television-saturated comics and magazines. Even the youngest are tele-consumers. Witness this year's demand for Teletubbies. This Christmas harassed parents are queuing for hours in the cold and rain to satisfy their toddlers' hunger for Laa Laa, Po and the others.

This sort of jaunty, hollow commercialism finds it way into almost every corner of children's culture. Take, for example, a recent issue of Cosmic – 'The BEST kid's magazine in the universe!' and published by H Bauer Publishing at £1.25 a copy. Prizes for the magazine's competitions include a 'Sony Combi TV And Video', a 'Sony Micro System' and a 'Sony Compact Discman, worth over £75'. Other prizes are toys based on the Jim Carrey film *The Mask* and colour files on Britian's (their spelling) 'best loved babes' – The Spice Girls!

Then there is *Big Time*, the Disney organisation's venture into British comic land. Among the cartoon strips are items on the latest (Disney) films, Hollywood star Jim

---

peever bed a grid on the ground for a game similar to hopscotch
inane mindless

Carrey and the younger end of the *EastEnders*, *Neighbours* and *Hollyoaks* casts. The Spice Girls feature too, naturally. And any youngster smart enough to 'unjumble' the words Oz Ebony to form the name of a 'top pop group' (how about Boyzone?) would win a 'pop-tastic hi-fi system' built into a giant Coca-Cola can worth £229.

So it seems that the superpowers of the children's world are now Telewood and Popistan. If it's not on the box or in the charts, it's not on. Infants of two and three pant for plastic versions of the characters and monsters they see on their screens. Our children's imaginations are inhabited by soap stars, Hollywood film actors, low-grade rock'n'rollers and acts of **contrived winsomeness** like the Spice Girls. And, of course, the Teletubbies.

This represents a serious, maybe even a profound, cultural **dislocation**. It means that our children's cultural agenda is no longer their own. It is being set by big-time showbiz players (some of them distinctly unsavoury) in New York, Los Angeles and London. None of the 10-year-olds out there are under the street lamps, organising a game of levey or kick the can. As never before, what they wear, what they do and how they respond is being decided in the boardrooms, executive suites and cutting rooms of Big Media.

All of which seems a long way from the rough and tumble of Pieter Bruegel's painting. And so it is. The days of cuddy gi'e wey, peevers and all the rest are over, probably for good. But perhaps every educationalist, teacher and parent in Scotland should have a copy of *Kinderspiele* pinned to the wall. It might remind us of just how much has been lost in one generation. And of the empty, money-spinning trash which we have allowed to take its place.

---

contrived winsomeness trying very hard to be sweet and likeable
dislocation a shift away from the way it was

The Billycart Era
by *Clive James*

This extract is interesting because although it is taken from something longer, its clear structure makes it a very entertaining story in its own right. As you read this extract you should focus upon:
- how the writer structures the account to create points of tension for the reader
- the various methods by which the writer creates humour
- the choices you think the writer might have made – for example, do you think certain aspects of the story might be exaggerated? (Remember that the title of the book is *'Unreliable Memoirs'*.)

This is an extract from the writer's autobiography. In this section he is writing about building and racing 'billycarts', or go-carts, in the streets around where he grew up in Kogarah, Australia. This is a story of ambition and disaster.

I could not build billycarts very well. Other children, most of them admittedly older than I, but some of them infuriatingly not, constructed billycarts of advanced design, with skeletal hard-wood frames and steel-jacketed ball-race wheels that screamed on the concrete footpaths like a diving **Stuka**. The best I could manage was a sawn-off fruit box mounted on a fence-paling spine frame, with drearily silent rubber wheels taken off an old pram. In such a creation I could go at a reasonable clip down our street and twice as fast down Sunbeam Avenue, which

---

Stuka a dive bomber that made a harsh, screeching sound

was much steeper at the top. But even going down
Sunbeam my billycart was no great thrill compared with
the ball-race models, which having a ground-clearance of
about half an inch and being almost frictionless were able
to attain tremendous **velocities** at low profile, so that to the
onlooker their riders seemed to be travelling downhill
sitting magically just above the ground, while to the riders
themselves the sense of speed was breathtaking.

After school and at weekends boys came from all over
the district to race on the Sunbeam Avenue footpaths.
There would be twenty or thirty carts, two-thirds of them
with ball-races. The noise was indescribable. It sounded
like the Battle of Britain going on in somebody's
bathroom. There would be about half an hour's racing
before the police came. Residents often took the law into
their own hands, hosing the grim-faced riders as they
went shrieking by. Sunbeam Avenue ran parallel to
Margaret Street but it started higher and lasted longer.
Carts racing down the footpath on the far side had a
straight run of about a quarter of a mile all the way to the
park. Emitting shock-waves of sound, the ball-race carts
would attain such speeds that it was impossible for the
rider to get off. All he could do was to crash reasonably
gently when he got to the end. Carts racing down the
footpath on the near side could go only half as far,
although very nearly as fast, before being faced with a
right-angle turn into Irene Street. Here a pram-wheeled
cart like mine would demonstrate its sole advantage. The
traction of the rubber tyres made it possible to negotiate
the corner in some style. I developed a **histrionic** lean-
over of the body and slide of the back wheels which got
me around the corner **unscathed**, leaving black smoking

---

velocities speeds
histrionic wildly exaggerated
unscathed unharmed

trails of burnt rubber. Mastery of this trick saved me from being **relegated** to the ranks of the little kids, than which there was no worse fate. I had come to depend on being thought of as a big kid. Luckily only the outstanding ball-race drivers could match my fancy turn into Irene Street. Others slid straight on with a yelp of metal and a shower of sparks, braining themselves on the asphalt road. One driver scalped himself under a bread van.

The Irene Street corner was made doubly **perilous** by Mrs Branthwaite's poppies. Mrs Branthwaite inhabited the house on the corner. She was a known witch whom we often **persecuted** after dark by throwing gravel on her roof. It was widely believed she poisoned cats. Certainly she was a great ringer-up of the police. In retrospect I can see that she could hardly be blamed for this, but her behaviour seemed at the time like irrational hatred of children. She was a renowned gardener. Her front yard was like the cover of a seed catalogue. Extending her empire, she had flower beds even on her two front strips, one on the Sunbeam Avenue side and the other on the Irene Street side – i.e. on both outside edges of the famous corner. The flower beds held the area's best collection of poppies. She had been known to phone the police if even one of these was **illicitly** picked.

At the time I am talking about, Mrs Branthwaite's poppies were all in bloom. It was essential to make the turn without hurting a single hair of a poppy's head, otherwise the old lady would probably drop the telephone and come out shooting. Usually, when the poppies were in bloom, nobody dared make the turn. I did – not out of

---

relegated put back down
perilous dangerous
persecuted persistently annoyed
illicitly illegally

courage, but because in my **ponderous** cart there was no real danger of going wrong. The daredevil leanings-over and the dramatic skids were just icing on the cake.

I should have left it at that, but got ambitious. One Saturday afternoon when there was a particularly large turn-out, I got sick of watching the ball-race carts howling to glory down the far side. I organised the slower carts like my own into a train. Every cart except mine was deprived of its front **axle** and loosely bolted to the cart in front. The whole assembly was about a dozen carts long, with a big box cart at the back. This back cart I dubbed the chuck-wagon, using terminology I had picked up from the **Hopalong Cassidy** serial at the pictures. I was the only one alone on his cart. Behind me there were two or even three to every cart until you got to the chuck-wagon, which was crammed full of little kids, some of them so small that they were holding toy koalas and sucking dummies.

From its very first run down the far side, my super-cart was a triumph. Even the adults who had been hosing us called their families out to marvel as we went steaming by. On the supercart's next run there was still more to admire, since even the top-flight ball-race riders had demanded to have their vehicles built into it, therefore heightening its tone, swelling its passenger list, and multiplying its already impressive output of decibels. Once again I should have left well alone. The thing was already famous. It had everything but a dining car. Why did I ever suggest that we should transfer to the near side and try the Irene Street turn?

With so much inertia the super-cart started slowly, but it accelerated like a piano falling out of a window. Long

---

ponderous slow and heavy
axle bar holding the wheels in place
Hopalong Cassidy a children's film about cowboys

before we reached the turn I realised that there had been a serious miscalculation. The miscalculation was all mine, of course, Sir Isaac Newton would have got it right. It was too late to do anything except pray. Leaning into the turn, I skidded my own cart safely around in the usual way. The next few segments followed me, but with each segment describing an arc of slightly larger radius than the one in front. First gradually, then with stunning finality, the monster lashed its enormous tail.

The air was full of flying ball-bearings, bits of wood, big kids, little kids, koalas and dummies. Most disastrously of all, it was also full of poppy petals. Not a bloom escaped the **scythe**. Those of us who could still run scattered to the winds, dragging our wounded with us. The police spent hours visiting all the parents in the district, warning them that the billycart era was definitely over. It was a police car that took Mrs Branthwaite away. These was no point waiting for the ambulance. She could walk all right. It was just that she couldn't talk. She stared straight ahead, her mouth slightly open.

---

scythe large-bladed tool used for cutting grass

Letter from Randolph Caldecott, March 1873

In this letter the writer conveys a sense of fun and excitement for the reader. He does this by observing the events in a detailed and humorous way which recreates the atmosphere of the occasion. As you read this text you should focus upon:

- the writer's lively and varied use of language to create pace and drama
- his unconventional use of punctuation for particular effect
- the various ways in which he uses humour.

In this letter, the writer describes a trip to watch the annual Boat Race between Oxford and Cambridge universities. However, he finds the spectators more interesting than the race itself. Caldecott was a painter and illustrator, which may explain his vivid and humorous description of the atmosphere.

My dear Will,

I never saw the University Boat Race before, and I very nearly never saw it again, as you shall hear.

So many reports of the race are written – a whole steamboat load of reporters following the race – that I may be allowed to let off a few remarks on the subject. Personal impression literally.

The morning was very foggy in town, the sun looking like a pink wafer. I got on board a steamboat, went about a hundred yards, when the vessel moored itself to a pier to wait for the departure of the fog. So then I took train, and the train took me up the riverside. Lovely day outside town. Miles of people and carriages. Lots of good-looking girls. Scores of minstrels, troubadours*, coco-nut and stick-throwing proprietors. Popping of champagne corks from the carriages. Hundreds of adventurous people in small boats and on river barges. Charming garden parties on pleasant lawns. Fat ladies on horseback. Swells in four-in-hand drags*. Cads in cabs. Beer served through the windows of the inns. Hardy pleasureseekers seated on broken-glass-bottle-topped walls. Nimble youths swarming trees, securing places of advantage at the ends of boughs, and then falling down to the heads of the pleased multitude. A few hand to hand contests. Much shoving. Bawling of police. Treading on toes. Upsetting of stands commanding fine views of the race. Hats off! Cheers. Here they come! There they go! Cambridge winning. Tide flows over osier* beds. Happy payers of 5/- each up to their knees in water. Wash of the steamers undermines respectable elderly gentlemen taking care of their plump partners. They struggle. They slip. Down they go. Damp just below the back of the waistcoat. Strong men carry timid people on their backs through the water. Foot in a hole. All roll over together. Jeers of the populace. A rush. Several benches and forms with rows of British ratepayers slide about in the mud. Clutching of neighbours. Lurch. Splash. Over they go. Swearing. All safe to land. Plenty for the money. Not only good view of the race; but wet legs

---

troubadours wandering poets
Swells in four-in-hand drags fashionable young men driving expensive carriages
osier small willow tree

and damp clothes – some wet and muddy all over.

So much for other people. I – after the race –
walked along the river bank and was soon in the
closest crush and squeezingest mob in which I was ever
a party – and I have been in a few. Between the
water and a high wall were a carriage road and
footpath. There was a close row of unhorsed vehicles
of every description; and a swaying, surging crowd of
all classes of folks moving each way. And in addition,
horsed carriages and people on horseback trying to
get along. Then did ladies scream and infants cry.
Then did protruding elbow find soft concealment in
yielding waistcoat, and tender faces unwilling repose
on manly bosoms. Corns were ground. Bonnets said
farewell to chignons*. Chests had no room to sigh, lips
that seldom swore spake grunted oaths, and unknown
forms were welded together and blended in sardine-
like harmony. Then slid the purse and fled the watch.
(A gentleman near me lost seventy pounds.)

I enjoyed the sight of the many thousands of
people, it was good fun to watch the manner of
passing away the time before the race. This was
about the best.

So you will observe that there is very much to be
seen besides the boat race.

We – that is Wales, Albert Victor, and myself – all
got home as soon as possible and felt better after a
good dinner.

I hope you are all well, and with kind regards to
each, remain, my dear William,

Yours faithfully
Randolph Caldecott

---

chignons hair pinned up at the back of the head

Letter from Jane Austen to her sister

This letter is full of observation and detail that give us a glimpse of a world very different from our own. As you read it, you should focus upon:

- the ways in which the writing reveals a sense of the writer's character
- the writer's use of humour in her descriptions of people
- the way the letter lets us understand something about the time it was written.

The writer is famous for her novels about life in 18th-century England. She particularly enjoyed what we might call 'people watching' and her books are full of funny and spiteful observations. This letter to her sister is full of gossip about people's behaviour and appearance. Some of the language she uses is unfamiliar, but the letter shows us how little has changed when it comes to people's interest in the social world around them.

---

20 November 1800

My dear Cassandra,

Your letter took me quite by surprise this morning, you are very welcome however, and I am very much obliged to you. Charles came yesterday morning. About two o'clock he walked in on a Gosport Hack.* — His feeling equal to such a fatigue is a good sign, and his finding no fatigue in it a still better. — We walked

down to Deane to dinner, he danced the whole Evening, and
today is no more tired than a gentleman ought to be. — Your
desiring to hear from me on Sunday will perhaps bring in you a
more particular account of the Ball than you may care for,
because one is prone to think much more of such things the
morning after they happen, than when time has entirely driven
them out of one's recollection. — It was a pleasant Evening,
Charles found it remarkably so, but I cannot tell why, unless
the absence of Miss Terry — towards whom his conscience
reproaches him with now being perfect indifferent — was a relief
to him. — There were only twelve dances, of which I danced
nine, and was merely prevented from dancing the rest by the
want of a partner. — We began at 10, supped at 1, and were at
Deane before 5. — There were but 50 people in the room; very
few families indeed from our side of the Country, and not many
more from the other. — My partners were the two St Johns,
Hooper Holder — and very prodigious — Mr Mathew, with
whom I called the last, and whom I liked the best of my little
stock. — There were very few Beauties, and such as there were,
were not very handsome. Miss Iremonger did not look well, and
Mrs Blount was the only one much admired. She appeared
exactly as she did in September, with the same broad face,
diamond bandeau, white shoes, pink husband, and fat neck. —
The two Miss Coxes were there; I traced in one of the remains
of the vulgar, broad featured girl who danced at Enham eight
years ago; — the other is refined into a nice, composed looking
girl like Catherine Bigg. — I looked at Sir Thomas

Gosport Hack a horse hired from the town of Gosport

Champneys and thought of poor Rosalie; I looked at his daughter and thought her a queer animal with a white neck. — Mrs Warren, I was constrained to think a very fine young woman, which I much regret. She has got rid of some part of her child, and danced away with great activity, looking by no means very large. — Her husband is ugly enough; uglier even than his cousin John; but he does not look so very old. — The Miss Maitlands are both prettyish; very like Anne; with brown skins, large dark eyes, and a good deal of nose. — The General has got the Gout, and Mrs Maitland the Jaundice. — Miss Debary, Susan and Sally all in black, but without any Statues, made their appearance, and I was as civil to them as their bad breath would allow me. They told me nothing new of Martha. — I mean to go to her on Thursday, unless Charles should determine on coming over again with his friend Shipley for the Basingstoke Ball, in which case I shall not go till Friday. — I shall write to you again however before I set off, and I shall hope to hear from you in the mean time. If I do not stay for the Ball, I would not on any account do so uncivil a thing by the Neighbourhood as to set off at that very time for another place, and shall therefore make a point of not being later than Thursday morning. — Mary said that I looked very well last night; I wore my aunt's gown and handkerchief, and my hair was at least tidy, which was all my ambition. —

I will now have done with the Ball; and I will moreover go and dress for dinner.

Yours affec. Sister
J. A.

Activities

Christmas at school

1 The writer remembers clearly the way his school was transformed in the days approaching Christmas. See if you can find examples of how the following aspects of school life seemed to change.

- the way the classrooms looked
- the way discipline was used
- the way the children spent their time.

2 Despite being almost 80 years old when he wrote this book, the writer describes the atmosphere and excitement through the eyes of a young child. Choose **two** quotations from the extract that you think show this well and explain why they are effective. An example has been done for you.

Quotation	How it conveys a sense of excitement
Fluttering coloured paper streamers, pom-poms, Chinese lanterns, and decorations were hung from walls and ceilings.	The writer creates a sense of movement and colour with the description of the streamers *fluttering*. There is a feeling that the school is full of decorations which have transformed it into a magical place.

3 The writer was born in 1916 and would have been at primary school in the early 1920s. In many ways, schools were very different then – for example, you would not expect to be thrashed at school now. However, in other ways schools have not changed. How many of the things that he describes do you remember from your own time at primary school?

4 Write a description of your primary school in the weeks before Christmas. Use carefully observed detail in the way that the writer of this extract has done and convey your sense of excitement. You could include:

- how the atmosphere changed
- how the school was decorated
- any parties, plays, concerts or performances you were involved in
- ways in which the teachers behaved differently
- special customs unique to your school.

You could start your writing: *As Christmas approached, the school was transformed into...*

My East End

1 In her opening paragraph, the writer says that when she was growing up children had *little purpose-built equipment*. Give several examples of what she might mean by this phrase.

2 This extract mentions about ten games played by children in East End streets. Make a list of them and put a tick next to those that you are familiar with and a cross next to those you have never played.

3 One street game, Release, is described in detail. Read it again, then write clear instructions for how to play it. Number them in order and include a diagram. You could start: *This game needs about 12 players split into two teams*.

4 The extract mentions rhymes that were used to decide if a player should be out of a game. Are these familiar to you? Do you remember any other rhymes or phrases that were only used in games? Work in small groups, then feed back your ideas to the class.

5 Some parts of this extract are written down directly from spoken accounts given to the author. This highlights the difference between written and spoken language. Copy the table below and use arrows to match each example to the correct feature.

Language feature	Example
• vague language • grammatical constructions that would be incorrect in writing • partial sentences • informal/slang language • simple, straightforward vocabulary	• *you'd spin a coin or whatever* • *We had an old ball and used our hands for bats.* • *Tire yourself out.* • *mates* • *Didn't cost nothing.*

6 Create a more up-to-date account of children's games to add to a similar book. In pairs, interview each other about games you played when you were younger, perhaps at primary school. Either tape the account or make notes, then write it up in the style of an oral account, like the ones in this extract.

Profiting from Child's Play

1 In the first four paragraphs, the writer compares his own childhood and the games he played to those he saw in a 400-year-old painting. Pick out **six** activities that appeared in the painting that he also played as a child.

2 In the paragraph that begins, *Which begs the question, why?*, the writer suggests three reasons why children these days no longer seem to play outside. What are they? Do you agree with him?

3 The writer feels strongly that children's lives seem to be rather empty, and he uses a variety of techniques to show this. In pairs, through discussion, match up the technique listed below with the appropriate example.

Technique	Example from the text
Negative language	*Why are our children and grandchildren so unfamiliar with all these venerable games and pastimes?*
Listing	*inane variety of pop music*
Disgust	*Adults had no part in it.*
Short sentences for impact	*Roaming the streets of Granton on clear frosty nights...*
Dramatic, sweeping statements	*This Christmas harassed parents are queuing for hours in the cold and rain to satisfy their toddler's hunger for Laa Laa, Po and the others.*
Description to create atmosphere	*In one generation the rich, vigorous and probably ancient children's culture of north Europe seems to have disappeared.*
Rhetorical questions	*skipping ropes, running across two rows of outstretched legs; leapfrog; dressing up...*

4 In many ways, the writer is very critical of the lives that modern children lead and of big businesses, which he thinks force children into behaving in particular ways. Copy the table below, which shows some of the points that he makes. In pairs, decide if you agree or disagree with him. Then work out a response to what he says, based on your own experience.

Key Point	Agree / disagree	Own response
Children don't know how to play games such as leapfrog, dressing up and hopscotch		
Children commit vandalism now because they don't know of other ways to amuse themselves		
Children are only interested in the superficial culture of television-based toys and comics		
Children are no longer capable of organising and thinking for themselves.		

5 Write a reply to the article, arguing against the writer's criticisms of children's lives, and drawing on the same techniques that he uses. Use examples from your own experience and build on the responses you made in Activity 4. Some useful phrases might be:

- *I disagree very strongly with…*
- *I have plenty of evidence from my own experience to…*
- *You suggest that…*
- *However…*
- *In response to this I would argue…*
- *On the other hand…*
- *An alternative way to look at this might be…*

The Billycart Era

1 The writer uses sound to convey the excitement and drama of the racing. Read the second paragraph and make a list of all the words and phrases connected with sound.

2 In the third paragraph the writer introduces us to the only adult in the story. Draw an outline of Mrs Branthwaite and around it write down what we find out about her. What is the most important thing he tells us about her? Why does he tell us this?

3 The writer tells this story in eight paragraphs and has structured it carefully to create maximum impact and tension. Below are summaries of the paragraphs, but they are in the wrong order. Draw a table like the one started on the next page and put the paragraphs in the correct order.

   a He introduces the character of Mrs Branthwaite and explains how proud she was of her garden.

   b He explains how billycarts were constructed and how his was not as exciting as other, more advanced designs.

   c He tells us how he organised the slower carts into a train.

   d He describes how the billycarts were raced on the footpaths and how, unlike the faster carts, his could negotiate corners.

   e The super-cart accelerates out of control and the writer realises he has made a miscalculation.

f We are told that Mrs Branthwaite's garden was at its best, with the poppies in full bloom.

g He describes the chaos of the crash and the effect it had on Mrs Branthwaite.

h He tells us how proud he was of his super-cart and that he wanted to make it even more impressive by trying to turn it.

Paragraph	Summary
1	He explains how billycarts were constructed and how his was not as exciting as other, more advanced designs.

4 Based on the ordering of the paragraphs you have completed, make a sketch of the shape of this story as if it were a graph line. How does the story build up slowly to a climax? Where does the climax of the story come? Do you think there is a sharp anticlimax?

5 The writer uses various types of humour in order to make his account entertaining. Some of them are listed below; try to find an example of each of the following from the text:

- visual humour
- exaggeration
- anticipation (we know something is going to happen)
- caricature (exaggerating a description of a person for comic effect).

6 The writer uses a range of literary techniques to tell his story. Think of an incident from your early childhood and write about it, using some of the techniques you have explored. Try to:

- give it an interesting structure with a clear and dramatic climax
- include some of the types of humour used in this extract
- use descriptive detail, such as sound, to build up the atmosphere and tension.

Letter from Randolph Caldecott, March 1873

1 As an artist, the writer was used to making quick sketches of things he observed and that is exactly what he does here with words. Look at the third paragraph and make a list of:

- the people he observes and the adjectives he uses to describe them, for example, adventurous people in small boats
- the sounds he includes in his description
- the words he uses to describe movement.

2 The writer uses language to reflect the pace, drama and humour of what he sees. Sometimes this involves breaking grammatical rules to achieve particular effects. Use the third paragraph to fill in the table on the next page.

Language feature	Example	Effect
Complete sentences at the opening of the description		
Use of incomplete sentences later in the description		
Use of alliteration (the same letter or sound at the start of words)		
Use of onomatopoeic language (words that imitate the sound they describe)		
Use of exclamation marks		
Use of repetition		

3 In the fourth paragraph, the writer describes being caught up and almost crushed in a crowd. Again, he uses language in interesting ways to describe the experience. Select **three** of the quotations below and explain why you think the writer uses them:

- *squeezingest*
- *swaying, surging crowd*
- *Then did ladies scream and infants cry*
- *forms were … blended in sardine-like harmony*
- *Then slid the purse and fled the watch.*

4 Using the literary techniques you have looked at in this letter, write to a friend describing a lively event or place that you have experienced.

Copy the idea of writing as a sketch that recreates the atmosphere, such as sports day, a dance, a fairground or concert.

Letter from Jane Austen to her sister

1 We might think that a country ball in 1800 was a rather dull affair, but the writer seems to have enjoyed the evening she describes. Read the statements below carefully and find a quotation from the extract to support each one.

- the writer didn't dance every dance, but only because no one asked her
- the ball finished late – she didn't get home until nearly 5 a.m.
- she was happy with her own appearance – even if she criticised everyone else's.

2 Jane's sister Cassandra hinted that her sister had a *fondness for disliking people*. Even when she seems on the surface to be complimentary about people, she cannot resist adding a criticism. Copy and complete the table below, showing what she has to say about these individuals.

Person	Writer's comments
	She tells us she is much admired but then adds she has a pink husband and a fat neck
The two Miss Coxes	
Sir Thomas Champney's daughter	
	She describes them as *prettyish*, with large dark eyes, but can't resist adding they have big noses
Mrs Warren's husband	
Miss Debary, Susan and Sally	

3 Work in pairs to build up a picture of the character of the
writer and her life from this letter. How does she spend
her time? What sort of relationship does she have with her
sister Cassandra and her brother Charles? Use **three** of the
adjectives below in your description.

**unkind   lively   funny   observant   arrogant
spiteful   clever**

4 Imagine you are Cassandra and have just received this
letter. Write a reply in which you comment on some of the
things your sister has told you. You could start: *Dear Jane,
I received your letter this morning and it made me smile...*

Comparing the extracts

The activities in this section all ask you to look at how writers
recreate or reflect on their past experiences. The activities
below ask you to draw some comparisons between the texts
in terms of:

- the purpose of the writing
- the way the purpose influences the style of the writing
- the ways writers use their experiences to form opinions.

The final discussion activity asks you to make some
judgements about the qualities of each of the extracts in this
section and come to some conclusions about whether they
are *literary* non-fiction.

1 Look again at the first three extracts in this section:
'Christmas at school', *My East End* and 'Profiting from
Child's Play'. These writers are all looking back at
childhood experiences, but for different purposes. Copy
the table on the next page and match each extract to its
purpose with an arrow.

Extract	Purpose
'Christmas at school'	To use examples from the past to persuade, present a point of view or opinion
My East End	To entertain by recreating a sense of place
'Profiting from Child's Play'	To inform, make a record or document the past

The varied purposes mean that the style of each piece is different. Identify a few sentences from each extract which you would describe as typical of the style of that extract. How are the writers using language differently? Think about:

- How each of them uses facts – for example, is this extract mainly fact or opinion or a mixture of both?
- The kind of vocabulary used – for example, is it descriptive, using adjectives and adverbs?
- Sentence length and structure – for example, does it use simple or complex sentences?
- How they use language to relate to the reader – for example, do they use rhetorical questions (questions asked for effect, rather than to get an answer, e.g. *How should I know?*)?
- Would you describe the style as formal or informal?

2 The writers of *My East End* and 'Profiting from Child's Play' clearly feel that children's lives at the start of the 21st century are less independent, less interesting and narrower than those of children in earlier decades.

Compare the points that the two writers make by deciding whether the ideas below are put forward by one or both of the writers. Add your own evidence in the form of a quotation.

- children were more creative and inventive in their play
- childhood was somehow happier
- children were less under the direct control of adults
- television and other elements of the mass media have made children grow up more quickly
- the streets were safer places to play than they are now.

3 Take each of the points outlined in question 2 and in pairs prepare your own response to it. Do you agree with what these older writers say, or are there aspects of this issue that they have misunderstood or ignored? It might be useful to start by brainstorming all the different ways in which you and younger children spend time.

4 Look again at *The Billycart Era*. Imagine that the writer has been asked to write a contribution to a book like *My East End* (a factual, documentary record rather than an autobiographical story). Based on the facts of his account of disaster on the Sunbeam Avenue footpaths, write his contribution. Remember you need to focus on facts and explanation. You could start: *Go-carts, or billycarts as we used to call them, were an important part of how we entertained ourselves. They were built …*

5 In working through these extracts, you have explored a range of features that make them interesting or distinctive. All the extracts are about things that really happened, so they all belong with non-fiction rather than fiction. The crucial question is, are they *literary* non-fiction?

In small groups, working on a copy of the grid on page 199, review each of the texts and decide which of the criteria for literary non-fiction each one meets. Then decide which extracts are definitely literary non-fiction and which ones you are less confident about. Be prepared to share your judgements. Remember that there are no right and wrong answers!

Section 4

Historic events: sharing the impact in a writer's account

This section looks at descriptions of devastating events. While reading the extracts, it may be helpful to keep the following questions in mind.

- How do different forms of writing convey events in different ways?
- How might different writers record the same event differently?
- How do writers craft their words to affect your feelings?
- How can writers of fact make use of techniques more commonly associated with fiction writing?

Extracts in this section

1 On the sinking of the *Titanic* by Charlotte Collyer
2 Newspaper report on the sinking of the *Titanic*
3 The wreck of the *Titanic* by Robert Ballard
4 Letter from Major Stubbs to his daughter
5 *Goodbye to All That* by Robert Graves
6 *The Girl in the Red Coat* by Roma Ligocka
7 *Words to Outlive Us* by Natan Zelochower

Why the extracts have been selected

Extracts 1–3 are perspectives on the sinking of the *Titanic*. All use emotion to convey the power of factual events.

Extracts 4 and 5 are accounts of World War I. Both writers adapted what they wrote to suit their audience.

Extracts 6 and 7 are records of atrocities in Polish ghettoes during World War II. Each writer crafts their writing to convey tension and drama.

The *Titanic*

Everyone is familiar with the disaster that befell the biggest ship in the world, the White Star liner *Titanic*, on its maiden voyage on 14 April 1912. The story still captures our imagination, but nothing could be as graphic or moving as the accounts of the people who lived through the tragedy. Two of these extracts were written around the time of the event, and the third shows how the story remains a source of fascination long after that fateful night.

On the sinking of the *Titanic* by Charlotte Collyer

In this extract the writer shows how the event seems insignificant at first, then builds up to reveal its full horror. As you read this extract you should focus upon:
* the use of detail to convey what was happening, such as the sounds heard after the collision
* the way the writer creates tension by building it up a little at a time.

The writer was travelling second-class on the Titanic *with her husband and eight-year-old daughter, Marjorie. They had left their home in Hampshire, hoping to start a new life in America. The writer's husband, Harvey, was drowned, but she and her daughter survived. This is how she later recounted their experiences to an American magazine.*

The sensation to me was as if the ship had been seized by a giant hand and shaken once, twice then stopped dead in its course. That is to say there was a long, backward jerk, followed by a shorter one. I was not thrown out of my berth and my husband staggered on his feet only slightly. We heard no strange sounds, no rending of plates and woodwork, but we noticed that the engines had stopped running. They tried to start the engines a few minutes later but after some coughing and rumbling there was silence once more.

Our cabin was so situated that we could follow this clearly. My husband and I were not alarmed. He said that there must have been some slight accident in the engine room and at first he did not intend to go on deck. Then he changed his mind, put on his coat and left me. I lay quietly in my berth with my little girl and almost fell asleep again. In what seemed a very few moments my husband returned. He was a bit excited then. 'What do you think,' he exclaimed. 'We have struck an iceberg, a big one, but there is no danger – an officer just told me so.' I could hear the footsteps of people on the deck above my head. There was some stamping and queer noises as if ships' tackle was being pulled about. 'Are the people frightened?' I asked quietly. 'No,' he replied, 'I don't think the shock woke up many of the second cabin, and few of those in the saloons have troubled to go on deck. I saw the professional gamblers playing with some of the passengers as I went by. Their cards had been jerked off the table when the boat struck, but they were gathering them up and had started their game again before I left the saloon.' The story reassured me. If these people at their cards were not worried, why should I be?

I think my husband would have retired to his berth but suddenly we heard hundreds of people running along the passageway in front of our door. They did not cry out, but the patter of their feet reminded me of rats scurrying through an empty room. I could see my face in the mirror opposite and it had grown very white. My husband too was pale and he stammered when he spoke to me. 'We had better go on deck and see what's wrong,' he said. I jumped out of bed and put a dressing gown over my nightdress. I hurriedly tied my hair back with a ribbon. By this time although the boat had not made any progress, it seemed to have tilted forward a little. I caught up my daughter just as she was in her nightgown, wrapped a White Star cabin blanket around her and started out of the door. My husband followed immediately behind. Neither of us took any belongings from the cabin and I remember that he even left his watch lying on his pillow. We did not doubt for an instant that we would return. When we reached the second cabin promenade deck we found a great many people there. Some officers were walking up and down. My husband stepped over to an officer – it was either Fifth Office Harold Lowe or First Officer Murdoch – and asked him a question. I heard him shout back: 'No, we have no searchlight but we have a few rockets on board. Keep calm! There is no danger.'

Our party of three stood close together. Suddenly there was a commotion near one of the gangways and we saw a **stoker** come climbing up from below. He stopped a few feet away from us. All the fingers on one hand had been cut off. Blood was running from the stumps and blood was spattered over his face and over his clothes. The red marks showed very clearly against the coal dust with which he was covered. I went over and spoke to him. I asked him if there was any danger. 'Danger?' he screamed at the top of his voice. 'I should just say so! It's hell down below. This boat will sink like a stone in ten minutes.'

He staggered away and lay down fainting with his head on a coil of rope. At this moment I got my first grip of fear – awful sickening fear. That poor man, with his bleeding hand and his speckled face brought up a picture of smashed engines and mangled human bodies. I hung on to my husband's arm and although he was very brave, and not trembling, I saw that his face was as white as paper. We realised that the accident was much worse then we had supposed, but even then, I and all the others about me of whom I have any knowledge did not believe that the *Titanic* would go down.

The officers were running to and fro shouting orders. I saw First Officer Murdoch place guards by the gangways to prevent others like the wounded stoker from coming on deck. How many unhappy men were shut off in that way from their chance of safety I do not know, but Mr Murdoch was probably right. He was a masterful man, astoundingly brave and cool. I had met him the day

---

stoker man who shovels coal into the ship's furnace

before when he was inspecting the second cabin quarters, and thought him a bull-dog of a man who would not be afraid of anything. This proved to be true. He kept order to the last, and died at his post. They say he shot himself. I do not know.

Those in charge must have herded us towards the nearest boat deck for that is where I presently found myself, still clinging to my husband's arm, and with little Marjorie beside me. Many women were standing with their husbands and there was no confusion. Then above the clamour of the people asking questions of each other, there came the terrible cry, 'Lower the boats! Women and children first.' Someone was shouting these last few words over and over again. 'Women and children first! Women and children first!' They struck utter terror into my heart and now they will ring in my ears until the day I die. They meant my own safety but they also meant the greatest loss I have ever suffered – the life of my husband.

Newspaper report from the *New York Call*, 16 April 1912

This is an interesting newspaper report because it combines fact with emotive language to increase its impact. As you read this report you should focus upon:

- the language the writer uses to present the facts and how this conveys the drama of the situation
- the way the report is structured to maximise the impact of the facts.

Today, details of a disaster like the sinking of the Titanic would be flashed around the world's television screens within minutes. However, in 1912 things happened more slowly and details of the tragedy were revealed over a number of days and weeks. Some early reports suggested that no lives had been lost and the ship had not in fact sunk. This report appeared in a New York newspaper four days after the event.

16th April 1912

New York Call

1500 persons hurled to death as monster liner *Titanic* is sunk by collision with mountain of ice

Enormous Mass Fatal to World's Greatest Steamship on Maiden Voyage, Despite Aid by Sister Ships

WIRELESS CALLS BRING AID TOO LATE

The greatest marine disaster in the history of the world occurred last Sunday night when the *Titanic*, of the White Star Line, the biggest and finest of steamships, shattered herself against an iceberg and sank, with 1500 of her passengers and crew in less than four hours.

Out of nearly 2200 people that she carried only 675 were saved, and most of these were women and children. They were picked up from small boats by the Cunarder *Carpathia*, which found, when she ended her desperate race against time, a sea strewn with wreckage of the lost ship and the bodies of drowned men and women.

Among the 1320 passengers of the giant liner were Col. John Jacob Astor and his wife; Isidor Straus; Maj. Archibald W. Butt, aide to President Taft; George W. Widener and Mrs Widener of Philadelphia; Mr and Mrs Henry S. Harper; William T. Stead, the London journalist, and many more whose names are known on both sides of the Atlantic. The news that few besides women and children were saved has caused the greatest apprehension as to the fate of these.

When the *Titanic* plunged headlong against the wall of ice at 10.30 p.m. (New York time) on Sunday night, her fate established that no modern steamship is unsinkable, and that all of a large passenger list cannot be saved in a liner's small boats. The White Star Line believed that the *Titanic* was practically invulnerable and insisted, until there was no doubting the full extent of the catastrophe, that she could not sink. The great ship was the last word in modern scientific construction, but she found the ocean floor almost as quickly as a wooden ship.

On her maiden trip, the *Titanic*, built and equipped at a cost of $10,000,000, a floating palace, found her graveyard. Swinging from the westerly steamship lane at the south of the Grand Banks of Newfoundland to take the direct run to this port she hurled her giant bulk against an iceberg that rose from an immense field drifted unseasonably from the Arctic. Running at high speed into that grim and silent enemy of seafarers, the shock crushed her bow. From a happy, comfortable vessel she was converted in a few minutes into a ship of misery and dreadful suffering.

Through rent plates and timbers, water rushed so swiftly that her captain, E.J. Smith, the admiral of the White Star fleet, knew there was no hope of saving her.

It has been many years since the world was left in such suspense and dread as following the first faltering calls for help from the crushed *Titanic*. At 10.30 p.m. on Sunday night, the *Virginian*, speeding on her way to Glasgow, picked up the White Star steamship's insistent, frantic **C.Q.D.**, the Marconi signal of distress and peril that clears the air of all lesser messages and stops ships at sea full in their tracks.

Dash by dash and dot by dot, the wireless operator of the *Virginian* caught the cry for help.

'Have struck an iceberg. Badly damaged. Rush aid.'

Seaward and landward, J.G. Phillips, the *Titanic's* wireless man, was hurling the appeal for help. By fits and starts – for the wireless was working unevenly and blurringly – Phillips reached out to the world, crying the *Titanic's* peril. A word or two, scattered phrases, now and then a connected sentence, made up the messages that sent a thrill of apprehension for a thousand miles east, west and south of the doomed liner.

C.Q.D. a general distress call to anyone listening

The wreck of the *Titanic* by Robert Ballard

In this extract the writer recounts a dramatic factual event, using characters in much the same way as a novelist might. He pays careful attention to the reactions and emotions of the people involved through what they say and how they respond to events. As you read this extract you should focus upon:

- the way the writer contrasts the characters and their reactions
- the way he builds tension by giving clues at different points
- the way emotions are used to convey the drama of the situation.

The writer is the deep-sea explorer who led the team that found the wreck of the Titanic *more than seventy years after it had sunk onto the Atlantic seabed. They used a small remote-controlled submarine called the* Argo *to locate the wreck, which lay two miles below the surface. The 'control van' that is referred to in the extract is on board the writer's ship the* Alvin, *and houses the monitors that show the images sent from the* Argo. *The team had almost given up their search, when the cameras revealed debris on the ocean floor.*

Down in the control van, video-tech Bill Lange turned to Stu Harris.

'What are we going to do to keep ourselves awake tonight?' he asked.

The video monitors scrolled the same monotonous image: soft grey mud, low rippling sand hills. It was 0048 hours, twelve minutes before one A.M.

Stu did not answer. His eyes were fixed on the screen. 'There's something,' he said quietly, pointing at the monitor.

Everyone in the van was suddenly alert.

Stu flipped switches, changing the monitor view from the forward-scanning camera to the down-looking zoom. A moment later, Stu burst with excitement. 'It's coming in!'

Bill Lange leaned close to the screen, then shouted, 'Wreckage!'

Stu Harris gazed at the flickering grey image. It was angular, probably steel, clearly debris from a ship, but there was no way of knowing if it was from *Titanic*. In 1912, the liner had sunk in the regular trans-Atlantic shipping lanes, but over the intervening years, so had scores of other ships, particularly during World War II when German U-boats had prowled these waters searching for helpless cargo ships. It was more likely that *Argo* had found the debris from one of the wartime wrecks than from *Titanic*.

As *Argo's* floodlights cast their full power, the crew in the van could distinguish twisted rusty pipes and fittings. The debris appeared considerably older than the wreckage at the *Thresher* and *Scorpion* sites. But how old was the question.

There was little doubt, however, that this material was large.

Lieutenant George Rey, the sonar operator, called out distinctly, 'I'm getting a hard contact.'

'Bingo!' cried Stu.

Argo passed beyond the metallic objects. The screen revealed only a few small glacial boulders.

The people in the van stared quizzically at each other, as Stu was rewinding the video tape to the 0048 time hack. Had they all seen the same thing? Then, at 0058 hours, more metallic debris, including unmistakable sheets of riveted hull plate, slid across the TV monitors.

There could be no doubt. Argo was gliding 30 feet above *Titanic's* debris field. Search line number nine had just entered the wedge of unsurveyed terrain that

Jean-Louis Michel's SAR sweep had missed a month before.

Now all manner of metallic wreckage flowed across the video monitors.

'Someone should go get Bob,' Bill Lange suggested.

But no one wanted to leave the van at this moment of triumph.

Then, at four minutes after one A.M., Stu Harris said, 'Let's go get Bob.' But still, there were no volunteers.

Finally, the ship's cook, John Bartolomei, who was visiting the van for the first time, volunteered to fetch me.

While the cook headed **aft** towards my cabin, the sketchy grey image of a circular object suddenly filled the screen. It was 0105 hours. *Argo* flew at 14.6 metres above the bottom, at a depth of 12,230 feet. In the bright floodlights, three smaller circular shapes appeared on the larger metallic face.

'A boiler?' Jean-Louis mused.

Bill Lange was practically jumping up and down. 'It's a boiler!' he yelled.

But Jean-Louis, ever the precise engineer, was cautious. He grabbed the book containing the 1911 *Shipbuilder* article on the construction of the *Titanic* and her sister ship *Olympic*. After flipping to the pictures of the huge boilers in their Belfast **foundry**, then studying the image on the screen, Jean-Louis spoke with conviction.

'Yes. It *ees* a boiler.'

John Bartolomei leaned into my cabin and spoke with a strange tone of suppressed excitement. 'Uh, the guys think you should come down to the van.'

There were only two things that would have caused them to interrupt my rest at this time: either we had a

---

aft towards the back of the ship
foundry factory where things are cast in metal

serious problem with the equipment, or they had found *Titanic's* debris field.

I dragged on my jumpsuit over my flannel pyjamas and scrambled down three decks, my boat shoes slipping on the damp stairs.

When I burst through the doorway of the van, Stu Harris rushed up to me, his face full of joy. The first word that registered was 'boiler'.

In the three minutes it had taken the cook to call me, *Argo* had indeed passed over and videotaped one of *Titanic's* twenty-nine gargantuan boilers, unmistakable from the three side-by-side circular vents on the top plate.

I was twanging with excitement, my eyes shooting around the van like a strobe, registering splintered images: the position of the plotline, the depth, the time, both here on the Atlantic and back in the States.

Stu was rewinding the videotape to replay the boiler image. Earle Young flew *Argo* steadily, his face neutral, determined to stay at his station, working well, while the others in the van exploded with our triumph.

Suddenly, the enormity of what had happened washed over me. The film crew was documenting this historic event, and I knew I should have some fitting words to say. I turned to Jean-Louis and clapped him on the shoulder. His dark eyes were moist, brimming with pride. We had found *Titanic*.

'It was not luck,' Jean-Louis said softly. 'We earned it.'

But I could only reply with stunned incredulity, 'God damn ... God damn.'

Argo had found *Titanic*, the **Golden Fleece** of undersea exploration.

Golden Fleece something desirable but difficult to find (from Greek mythology; it was sought and won by Jason, travelling in his ship, the *Argo*)

Letter from Major Stubbs to his daughter

In this letter the writer has deliberately distorted the truth, presenting a particular version of it for a specific audience. He uses humour and images that are not normally associated with war. As you read this extract you should focus upon:

- the way the writer explains his situation through his choice of images, such as describing the soldiers as 'rabbits'
- how his writing is crafted to make it accessible to a young reader.

The writer was a major in the Royal Artillery, fighting on the Western Front in World War I. Letters were important as they were the soldiers' only contact with their families. Fighting on the Western Front was ferocious, and the writer would have experienced some horrifying situations. However, in this letter to his daughter, he tries to tell her about life in the trenches without revealing the true picture.

My dear little Katherine

Many thanks for your nice letter which I received yesterday. It was good of you to write such a nice letter & in such good writing. I gave your love to Capt. Hedley & Mr Burnley, but Mr Ingham and Mr Harris were both jealous. We live here more like rabbits than anything else & we have a lookout rabbit with glasses & a whistle who blows

3 blasts when he sees a German aeroplane then we all dive below & remain there until our lookout blows one blast. The German aeroplanes have a horrid habit of coming out just as our dinner & tea is being brought up to the Battery* with the result that the men carrying the meals have to squat down perhaps 100 yards away. We sit in our rabbit holes & peep out at our dinners while the dinners get cold. It is very annoying of them & is altogether a bad habit but three days ago our airmen went up after one of the Germans & shot him down, he also did the same thing with another the day before yesterday so that is two less anyway to bother us.

I am very well indeed & really am liking the life, if only we don't get too many shells at us. I am sending you a small piece of a shell which came to call yesterday. We were sitting having tea when we heard him & two friends coming, they whistle as they come to show how cheerful they are, this particular one sailed over just beyond the end of the Battery & burst right in the middle of the road 200 yards or so behind. There was a French ambulance coming along the road at the time, the shell must have missed it by inches as it burst only 10 yards behind it, the horse took no notice at all, a Frenchmen had the top of his finger blown off & the French surgeon some distance away got it in the leg. One of the other shells burst quite

---

Battery a fortified emplacement for heavy guns

close to another Battery but hurt no one.

    I went out afterwards & found this piece of shell which you should keep as a souvenir. Some day I will tell you the name of the place. The only other damage done was a blackbird killed which one of our men found & the road with a big hole in it, which we repaired as our wagons use it. We are ordering things for the men to be sent out weekly from Fortnum & Mason so except for a slab or two of chocolate & occasionally a cake I really don't want anything at present. I could do with another dozen drawing pins. We are now getting enough to eat if only the horrid German aeroplanes will leave us alone to eat it. You see it is very important that the German aeroplanes should not be able to see where we are as if they do they will quickly begin to shell us out & we would then have the bother of finding another position & digging our rabbit holes again & of planting a new plantation around the grass, so we are very careful. I have to preside* at a Court Martial* tomorrow which I am not looking forward to at all. Give my best love to Mummy & heaps to yourself. I know you will be good & will make Mummy happy.

Your own,
Daddy

---

preside to be at the head of
Court Martial a military court where soldiers are tried

Goodbye to All That
by *Robert Graves*

In this extract from his autobiography, the writer tells the reader about life in the trenches. His attitude to the war is revealed through what he chooses to write about and his stark presentation of events. As you read this extract you should focus upon:

- the writer's use of bleak and unemotional language
- the way he presents the people he writes about, showing admiration or contempt through his selection of detail.

The writer was a young officer in World War I. The horrors he witnessed left him shell-shocked and haunted him throughout his life. He was bitter and angry about what he saw as a terrible waste of human life and the incompetence of those in command.

In this extract he describes going into no-man's land (the area between the British and German trenches) to rescue the wounded, some of whom had been lying injured in the mud for hours. He contrasts their bravery with the indifference of the senior officers who seem to have little idea of what the men have experienced.

My memory of that day is hazy. We spent it getting the wounded down to the dressing-station, spraying the trenches and dug-outs to get rid of the gas, and clearing away the earth where trenches were blocked. The trenches stank with a gas-blood-**lyddite**-latrine smell. Late in the afternoon we watched through our field-glasses the advance of reserves under heavy shell-fire towards

---

lyddite an explosive

Loos and Hill 70; it looked like a real breakthrough. They were troops of the New Army division, whose staff we had **messed** with the night before. Immediately to the right of us we had the Highland Division, whose exploits on that day Ian Hay has celebrated in *The First Hundred Thousand*; I suppose that we were 'the flat caps on the left' who 'let down' his comrades-in-arms.

At dusk, we all went out to get in the wounded, leaving only sentries in the line. The first dead body I came upon was Samson's, hit in seventeen places. I found that he had forced his knuckles into his mouth to stop himself crying out and attracting any more men to their death. Major Swainson, the second-in-command of the Middlesex, came crawling in from the German wire. He seemed to be wounded in lungs, stomach, and one leg. Choate, a Middlesex second-lieutenant, came back unhurt; together we bandaged Swainson and got him into the trench and on a stretcher. He begged me to loosen his belt; I cut it with a **bowie-knife** I had bought at Béthune for use during the battle. He said: 'I'm about done for.'* We spent all that night getting in the wounded of the Royal Welch, the Middlesex, and those Argyll and Sutherland Highlanders who had attacked from the front trench. The Germans behaved generously, I do not remember hearing a shot fired that night, though we kept on until it was nearly dawn and we could see plainly; then they fired a few warning shots, and we gave it up. By this time we had recovered all the wounded, and most of the

---

messed ate
bowie-knife a long knife that has a double-edged blade at the point

* Major Swainson recovered, and was back at the Middlesex Depot after a few weeks. On the other hand, Lawrie, a Royal Welch quartermaster-sergeant back at Cambrin, was hit in the neck that day by a spent machine-gun bullet which just pierced the skin, and died of shock a few hours later.

Royal Welch dead. I was surprised at some of the attitudes in which the dead stiffened – bandaging friends' wounds, crawling, cutting wire. The Argyll and Sutherland had seven hundred casualties, including fourteen officers killed out of the sixteen who went over; the Middlesex, five hundred and fifty casualties, including eleven officers killed.

Two other Middlesex officers besides Choate came back unwounded; their names were Henry and Hill, recently commissioned second-lieutenants, who had been lying out in shell-holes all day under the rain, sniping and being sniped at. Henry, according to Hill, had dragged five wounded men into a shell-hole and thrown up a sort of parapet with his hands and the bowie-knife which he carried. Hill had some platoon-sergeant beside him, screaming with a stomach wound, begging for **morphia**; he was done for, so Hill gave him five pellets. We always carried morphia for emergencies like that.

Choate, Henry, and Hill, returning to the trenches with a few stragglers, reported at the Middlesex headquarters. Hill told me the story. The colonel and the adjutant were sitting down to a meat pie when he and Henry arrived. Henry said: 'Come to report it, sir. Ourselves and about ninety men of all companies. Mr Choate is back, unwounded, too.'

They looked up dully. 'So you've survived, have you?' the colonel said. 'Well, all the rest are dead. I suppose Mr Choate had better command what's left of "A" Company: the bombing officer will command what's left of "B" [the bombing officer had not gone over, but remained with headquarters]; Mr Henry goes to "C" Company. Mr Hill to "D". The Royal Welch are holding the front line. We are

---

morphia old name for morphine, a drug used to relieve pain, which is lethal in large doses

here in support. Let me know where to find you if you're needed. Good night.'

Not having been offered a piece of meat pie or a drink of whisky, they saluted and went miserably out.

The adjutant called them back. 'Mr Hill! Mr Henry!'

'Sir?'

Hill said that he expected a change of mind as to the propriety with which hospitality could be offered by a regular colonel and adjutant to temporary second-lieutenants in distress. But it was only: 'Mr Hill, Mr Henry, I saw some men in the trench just now with their shoulder-straps unbuttoned and their equipment fastened anyhow. See that this does not occur in future. That's all.'

Henry heard the colonel from his bunk complaining that he had only two blankets and that it was a deucedly cold night.

Choate, in peacetime a journalist, arrived a few minutes later; the others had told him of their reception. After he had saluted and reported that Major Swainson, hitherto thought killed, was wounded on the way down to the dressing-station, he boldly leaned over the table, cut a large slice of meat pie and began eating it. This caused such a surprise that no further conversation took place. Choate finished eating his meat pie and drank a glass of whisky; saluted, and joined the others.

The Girl in the Red Coat
by *Roma Ligocka*

In this extract the writer communicates the fear of a child caught up in events she doesn't understand. She does this by writing from a child's perspective, often using simple language and focusing on the immediate surroundings. As you read this extract you should focus upon:

- the effect of writing in the present tense
- the use of sound to build up tension
- the way she writes about frightening things simply, using straightforward vocabulary.

The writer's family were Jewish and lived in the Polish city of Krakow during World War II. Jews were rounded up by the Nazis and made to live in overcrowded conditions in a particular area of the city; this became known as the Krakow Ghetto. They lived in terror of being sent away to concentration camps such as Treblinka; many died from disease and starvation. In this extract, the writer describes how she and her family lived and the fear they experienced as their neighbours were taken away by German soldiers.

Still more people are now living in our house. Four instead of three people per window, my father said to my mother. Why did he say that? Anyway, nobody looks out of the window. Even I don't any more. Because it is forbidden now; the punishment is death. My mother warned me that anyone who opens a window or looks outside is going to be shot by the Germans. That's because our house borders on the **Aryan** residential district.

Aryan non-Jewish

There are two windows in the dark room where we sleep. My crib is gone, I now share a bed with my parents. It's warmer there, even though I often feel that I can't get any air, that I'm suffocating. The room has a sweetish smell. The air is stale and heavy.

The sewing machine isn't here any more either. The new people now sleep in the spot where it used to stand beneath the window. I miss the reassuring clatter of the sewing machine. Grandmother sews by hand now. Her knobbly fingers are quick and skilful. She sews dresses for people and mends their things. For that we get a little bread or tea or a handful of flour.

We sit in the dark kitchen and wait. Like rabbits in a burrow. My grandmother once told me about rabbits. They're small, soft animals with long ears and they can run very fast when they're being chased. They get chased most of the time. Then they quickly run into their underground holes and they're safe there.

I'd like to see a rabbit one day.

I keep hearing a new German word, 'AUSSIEDLUNG.' It means 'resettlement', but I don't know what that means, and Grandmother doesn't want to explain it to me. Everybody is constantly talking about it. I sense how afraid people are when they talk about it; it must be something terrible, this word.

I see my father only rarely now, and my mother's face looks grey. When she's home she stuffs food into my mouth. There's no time for anything else. Luckily I have my grandmother.

It is night, and they're coming to get us.

At least, that's what I think whenever I hear their boots on the stairs, their shouting, and the harsh barking of the dogs. Then I quickly make myself invisible. Will they find me? My heart is pounding in the darkness. The pounding is much too loud. They're going to hear it.

But they don't find me, not this time. They bang on the door; the dogs are panting. '**KENNKARTEN**!' they yell. They take the fat man with the beard who always snores so loudly at night and also the woman who dipped my head into the bowl. And the twins from upstairs; I sometimes saw them on the staircase. Even though I hold my breath and hide under the blanket like a rabbit, I can hear everything. The sobbing and pleading of the woman. And the wailing protest of the fat man, the rapid shuffling of his feet while he hurriedly packs his suitcase. The twins cry softly.

Then they are gone. It's over, and I'm relieved they didn't find me. I want to snuggle up to my mother, but she is stiff with fear. Is she dead? I tug her sleeve. 'Go to sleep now, Roma,' she whispers. The sound is as hollow as if it came out of a tunnel or a deep well. I don't dare say anything, don't dare to move, to breathe. I have to go to sleep. But then I hear them again. It isn't over yet. They are continuing their search in the next house, and in the one after that, and the one after that. People scream, dogs bark, men shout. It goes on like that all through the night.

In the early dawn, still half asleep, I hear the tramping of feet in the street, mixed with the shouts of the Germans.

LOS, LOS! **RAUS**, RAUS! **WEITER**! **SCHNELL**, SCHNELL!

Where are they all going? There are so many feet, big ones and small ones.

Slowly the sound of the tramping feed recedes; the barking of the dogs and the yelling fades, seems far away now. Maybe they'll come back to get me. It isn't over.

It's only the beginning.

Kennkarten identity cards
Los, raus, weiter, schnell move, get out, quickly

Words to Outlive Us
by *Natan Zelichower*

In this extract the writer conveys danger and panic by using a range of literary techniques. He is concerned not only to tell us what happened, but also to make us remember. As you read this extract you should focus upon:
- imagery, such as the description of the Gestapo officer as a bird of prey
- his use of other literary techniques such as alliteration, to create tension.

Natan Zelichower lived in the Jewish quarter of Warsaw, Poland, during the early part of World War II. Here he describes what it was like. In 1942, during the deportations of Jewish people, he lost both his wife and daughter, who were probably sent by the Nazis to the extermination camp at Treblinka. He was sent to a succession of concentration camps and was finally liberated from Buchenwald in April 1945. In this extract he describes the fear and tension of life in the Warsaw Ghetto under German occupation.

The people of the ghetto street formed one huge mass of castaways doomed to extinction, subsisting on a daily diet of anguished news and heart-wrenching notices. With its relentless reports of dead and dying friends and acquaintances, the street served as a constant **memento mori**, a terrible whip in the hand of a merciless executioner, flogging into **sobriety** any drunken hopes for a better tomorrow. But the street was also a true life-

---

memento mori (Latin) a reminder of death
sobriety soberness or clear thinking

giving artery. Shadowy figures emerged from the depths of the blackened city to feed off the street like **leeches**, and these in turn fed others, even to the point of nourishing **delusions** of a bright future built on easy living and abundant earnings.

Raw nerves cried out at the slightest touch. The most trivial matter would set women crowded around a kitchen stove to quarrelling. Every pot became the subject of a spat, every spoon sparked anger, every child's cry triggered a mother's sharp reaction. The ghetto lived in a constant tense clamour that grew worse with every piece of bad news and rarely if ever was silenced. Even the seemingly quiet nights only muffled but did not still this unbroken lament.

Everyone stayed alert. No one left home without first checking, 'What's it like out today?' Once outside, people focused trained eyes on their surroundings, searching for danger. Pedestrians traded words of warning that could suddenly shift the direction of traffic. Mere mention of a threat, the slightest gesture, could send a crowd of several thousand back inside, leaving the street empty and bare.

Danger could swoop down like a hawk. A black limousine would pull up at a street corner; a Gestapo officer would step out and casually survey the crowd. He would choose his victims, summon them with his finger, shove them into the car, and speed off toward the destroyed buildings on Dzielna Street, just opposite the Pawiak prison. There they would be subjected to a meticulous search and then shot in the head, while the car would return to the ghetto in search of new prey. This private hunting became a favourite sport among the dignitaries of the new regime in need of immediate financial relief. If they appeared on a street the traffic would slow down, although it never stopped altogether. After the limousine left, people

---

leeches creatures that suck blood
delusions false impressions

would diligently inquire who had been taken away – and then return to business, trading, shouting, haggling, consoling ... and waiting for the next black limousine.

During the night, soldiers would make the rounds of certain buildings accompanied by members of the **SP**; they would pound on doors using their rifle butts and nightsticks. Dozens of men whose names had been listed in advance would be dragged from their homes. These dazed, terrified victims would be led to some side street, lined up against a wall, and gunned down on the spot. Then the perpetrators would briskly ring the doorbells of the buildings nearest the corpses and order the **concierges** to stack the bodies in the entranceways and wash the blood off the pavement. A few hours later, crowds of people would step over the same spot completely unaware of what had taken place there. The only news of these incidents travelled through word of mouth, as people passed along the victims' names – at least for a day or two, until the next execution.

The Jews did not believe in their own extinction. At the very centre of their 'spiritual refuge' sat God, who, having led them through the Red Sea, would surely knock down the walls of the ghetto. While the executions filled people with terror and wrenched their hearts with fear, there was always some space left for reasoning: Methods such as this might enable the Germans to eliminate a few thousand or, let's say, even tens of thousands, but surely not half a million people! Logically speaking then, since not everyone inside the ghetto was doomed, each person had a chance of escaping alive. And the best defence against the executions was faith – an unwavering faith in divine protection, along with **vigilance** and cleverness to avoid getting caught in a roundup. In time, though, none of these defences could withstand the cunning techniques devised by the Germans.

SP secret police
concierges caretakers
vigilance watchfulness

Activities

On the sinking of the *Titanic*

1 One way in which the writer creates tension in this writing is by showing how quickly people move from calm curiosity to panic. Use a table like the one below to track how this happens.

Paragraph	Reactions/emotions	Evidence
1	Although they recognise the power of what has happened, there is no indication that they panic.	• It felt as if the ship had been seized and shaken by *a giant hand*. • They don't hear any strange sounds, only silence.
2		

2 One way in which the writer brings her account to life is through the use of detail. On a photocopy of the text, highlight the things that you think make her writing particularly vivid. Then choose **four** of the things you have highlighted and say why she mentions them. For example, *'I could see my face in the mirror opposite and it had grown very white'* – *I think this image shows that although on the surface she is not worried, she is in fact frightened by the events.*

3 Another way in which the writer makes her writing interesting is by using language we are more likely to associate with fiction than non-fiction. Find at least **two** examples where she uses similes or metaphors to express her ideas. Explain why you think she used them.

4 This is a good example of literary non-fiction because the writer has used a range of literary techniques to record a factual event. Try these out in a piece of your own writing: think of a time when you have felt frightened and write about it in two stages:

   a Outline the event in a few bullet points, with no detail or indication of your feelings or emotions.

   b Now develop this into a more crafted piece of work. Start, as in this extract, by making the incident seem insignificant and then build it up. Include:

     • carefully selected detail
     • development of emotions
     • similes and metaphors to express ideas.

Newspaper report from the *New York Call* 16th April 1912

1 This report is typical of its time in that it combines fact and emotive language in a powerful way in order to convey the drama of the event. Using a whole page, copy out the table below. Then re-read the report carefully and collect as many examples as you can of each stylistic feature.

Factual information including numbers for dramatic effect	Use of contrasts
Ship sank in less than four hours	*The great ship was the last word in modern scientific construction, but she found the ocean floor almost as quickly as a wooden ship.*
Use of superlatives	**Use of powerful verbs and adjectives**
greatest marine disaster	1500 persons **hurled** to death

2 A modern newspaper account of this event might use sub-headings as mini-headlines to break up the story into smaller chunks. Suggest **five** sub-headings that could be used at different points in this article. Each one should be not more than five words long.

3 Read the last four paragraphs again (starting at *It has been many years ...*). Choose four phrases that the writer uses to recreate the tension and panic of the wireless operator. Why do you think the article ends in this way?

4 How does this report convey what happened to the *Titanic* and its passengers in a dramatic and powerful way? You should write about:

- the way the *Titanic* is described
- the way the iceberg is described
- the use of statistics
- the use of emotive language
- the way the article ends.

The wreck of the *Titanic*

1 At first the team examining the pictures being sent back from the seabed are not sure they have found the *Titanic*. Gradually the clues are fitted together like a jigsaw. Write out the clues listed below in the order in which they appear in the text:

- sheets of riveted hull plate
- one of the boilers from the engine
- angular steel debris
- twisted, rusty pipes and fittings
- the material was large
- metallic wreckage.

2 Which of these is the most important in identifying the wreck of the *Titanic*? How do the explorers confirm that what they have found is from the *Titanic*?

3 The writer conveys the tension and excitement of the discovery through the reactions of the team, who respond in different ways. Work in pairs. Copy the table below and note evidence for each of the emotions listed. You may need to check the meaning of some words in a dictionary.

Emotion	Team member	Evidence
Boredom	Bill Lange	He doesn't know how he is going to keep awake through the night.
Excitement		
Curiosity		
Elation		
Pride		
Incredulity		

4 Despite the huge amount of excitement and emotion generated by the discovery of the wreckage, the announcement made by the writer at a press conference had to be calm, controlled and factual. Based on the account you have just read, write the short press statement he could have made when he came ashore. Plan your ideas and decide on the key points you want to make. You could begin: *At just after two a.m., local time, the cameras of our submarine Argos revealed…*

Letter from Major Stubbs to his daughter

1 What clues do we have about Katherine's age?

2 Collect as many examples as you can that show how the writer uses language to make things that are potentially dangerous or unpleasant seem less so. Make a copy of the table below to record your ideas.

What he writes	What he is describing
'We sit in our rabbit holes'	The soldiers in the trenches

3 Why do you think the writer chooses to describe the soldiers as rabbits? What kind of story is likely to feature animal characters rather than humans?

4 In the third paragraph the writer recounts an incident in which they were shelled by the Germans.

a What details does he include that suggest he has adapted the account for his daughter?

b What do you think might have really happened?

5 Throughout this letter the writer makes the war seem like a game. Some people might argue that he is wrong to give a child the impression that war is harmless fun.

Write a short script in which you interview the writer about why he decided to write this letter as he did. What might he say in response to the accusation that he was presenting war as a game in which no one got hurt?

Goodbye to All That

1 a How would you describe the tone and style of this
  extract? Copy out the list below and place a tick, a
  cross or write 'unsure' next to each. Then choose two
  you have ticked and two you have crossed and provide
  a quotation to illustrate each one. An example has been
  done for you:

  - stark
  - descriptive
  - emotional
  - emotionless
  - matter of fact ✓
  - bleak
  - simple
  - complex
  - sentimental

  The extract seems matter of fact in places, for example:
  '"So you've survived, have you?" the colonel said.'

  b Compare your list with a partner's and discuss points
  you are uncertain about. Why is it difficult to decide?

2 Although the writer never uses the words *brave* or
  courageous, there are several examples of men behaving
  with great bravery in this extract. See how many you can
  find and write them down. Why do you think the writer
  does not comment on the men's behaviour?

3 Find the section where the writer gives details about the
  number of deaths that resulted from this single incident.
  Again, he makes no comment of his own. Why does he
  include these statistics?

4 Only three out of fourteen officers from the Middlesex
  regiment came back from this attack: Choate, Henry and
  Hill. How were they treated when they reported to the
  colonel?

5 What does the way this extract is written tell you about
  the writer's attitude to the war? Think about:

  - the tone and style of the writing
  - the way he shows how much he admires the soldiers
  - the way he uses statistics
  - how he presents those who are not directly involved in
    the fighting, such as the colonel and the adjutant.

The Girl in the Red Coat

1 Although the writer is an adult recalling things that happened to her as a child, she tries to write from a child's perspective. Work in pairs, and suggest four ways in which she does this. Two examples have been done for you.

- *The writer uses mainly simple sentences with few complex sentences. This echoes the kind of language a child would use and is more like speech than writing.*
- *The writer uses the present tense (We <u>sit</u> in the dark kitchen and wait) and this adds to the immediacy of what is happening.*

2 Roma's world has changed greatly in a short time. Copy out the table below and use the first half of the text to identify as many changes as you can. You may need to make logical guesses about her life before the Germans forced the Jews of Krakow to live in the ghetto.

Before	After
Roma knew who lived in the neighbouring rooms	The house is occupied by more and more people who she doesn't know

3 In this situation the family are likened to rabbits. From the extract, find **three** ways in which they are like rabbits and one way in which they are not.

4 Although the writer does not actually see the German soldiers, she manages to convey the horror of what they do. Using the second part of the extract, make a list of the ways in which she does this. The list has been started for you:

- *The soldiers always seem to come at night.*
- *They have dogs with them which suggests people are being hunted.*

5 One of the ways in which tension is created in this extract is through the use of sound. Identify all the sounds that the writer hears in the second part of the extract. Do they have anything in common?

6 Most of us have never experienced anything this terrifying, but all children experience confusion and sometimes fear about things they do not understand. Think of a time when you were frightened and describe the incident through the eyes of a young child, making it dramatic and immediate for your reader by using some or all of the following features:

- write in the present tense
- use mainly simple rather than complex sentences
- show the things you are confused about by using questions
- make use of sounds you can hear as a way of building tension.

Words to Outlive Us

1 In the first paragraph the writer tries to show how central the street was to people's lives. One idea he uses is the metaphor of the street as a *'terrible whip in the hands of a merciless executioner, flogging into sobriety any drunken hopes for tomorrow'*. In this way he gives us a sense of how life on the street brutally destroyed any hope that things might get better. He uses two other ideas or metaphors about the ghetto street:

- the idea that the people are 'a huge mass of castaways'
- the street as 'a life-giving artery'.

Take each of these ideas and explain what it tells you about street life in the ghetto and what it may have meant for the people who lived there.

2 In the second paragraph the writer describes how tense life is and how even the smallest incident can quickly turn into something more serious. Write a paragraph about how he does this. You might look for:

- all the different words associated with sounds
- how the people behave
- words that are repeated
- how he uses alliteration (the same letter or sound at the start of words).

3 The writer starts the fourth paragraph with the idea that the people are like defenceless animals who are picked off by a ruthless and powerful enemy. Imagine you lived on these streets. In what ways would you be made to feel vulnerable?

4 As well as being an interestingly crafted piece of writing, this is also an important historical document. The title of the book that this extract came from is *Words to Outlive Us*.

- What do you think the writer wanted to achieve by writing an account of these events?
- Why was the book given this title?
- Why did he choose to write in such a literary style?

Comparing the extracts

The texts in this section give different perspectives on the same subject matter. The following activities ask you to draw some comparisons between the texts in terms of:

- the purpose of the writing
- the audience for the writing
- the way the writing is crafted according to purpose and audience
- the impact and significance the writing has on you as a reader.

The final discussion activity asks you to make some judgements about the qualities of each of the extracts in this section and come to some conclusions yourselves about whether they are *literary* non-fiction.

1 Robert Graves and Major Stubbs give quite different ideas
   about life in the trenches in World War I. Robert Graves
   wanted to make an accurate record of his experiences,
   whereas Major Stubbs is writing to his young daughter
   and clearly wants to protect her from the realities of war.

   a Imagine that Major Stubbs also keeps a diary in which
   he records the same events more realistically. Re-read
   both texts and then write a diary entry for Major Stubbs
   in which he is able to give an honest account of one of
   the events he describes in his letter.

   b Pick out the ways in which the two writers describe the
   Germans. What do you think this shows about the
   different ways the two men thought about their enemy?

2 Look at the extracts *The Girl in the Red Coat* and *Words
   to Outlive Us*.

   a The two extracts about life in the wartime ghettos are
   written from different perspectives. Natan Zelichower
   records his experiences as an adult, and Roma Ligocka
   describes events through the eyes of a child. Explain
   how is this shown in the writing. You need to look at:

   • the vocabulary and sentence structure used in each
     account
   • the way the behaviour of the soldiers is described
   • the different places and settings written about
   • the way each writer describes their feelings and their
     reactions to what is happening to them.

   b Despite important differences, there are similarities too.
   How would you know that these writers are describing
   similar experiences? Think about:

   • what actually happens
   • how the writers use sound to convey a sense of fear
   • the idea of people being hunted like animals.

   c Both writers would say that they had recorded their
   experiences truthfully. In pairs, discuss which one you
   find the most frightening and convincing.

3 Writing about the fear, death and conflict involved in war is difficult and writers use different approaches to convey their emotions and ideas. Some might choose a matter-of-fact approach to mask the horror, others might use humour. A writer might include detailed description or might deliberately avoid detail and encourage readers to use their imagination. Look again at the four extracts concerned with war:

- Letter from Major Stubbs to his daughter
- *Goodbye to All That*
- *The Girl in the Red Coat*
- *Words to Outlive Us*.

a Choose **two** of the extracts. How do these writers convey the horror of their experiences? In your answer, consider the following questions:

- Do they take a matter-of-fact approach that masks the horror?
- Do they use humour, and if so, why?
- Do they choose to include detailed description, or do they avoid detail to encourage readers to use their imagination?

b Which text did you find most powerful and why?

4 In working through these texts you have explored a range of features that make them interesting or distinctive. All of the texts are about things that have really happened, so they all belong with non-fiction rather than fiction. The crucial question is, are they *literary* non-fiction?

In small groups, working on a copy of the grid on page 199, review each of the texts and decide which of the criteria for literary non-fiction each one meets. Then decide which extracts are definitely literary non-fiction and which ones you are less confident about. Be prepared to share your judgements. Remember that there are no right and wrong answers!

Section 5

Fact and fiction: exploring why a writer chooses to blur 'truth'

This section asks some of the big questions about literary non-fiction:

- How do writers select and manipulate facts to convey their own version of the truth?
- How do writers stretch conventions, style and structure to make difficult ideas more accessible?
- What are the effects of deliberately mixing fact and fiction?

Extracts in this section

1 *My Side* by David Beckham
2 *How Do You Want Me?* by Ruby Wax
3 *Billy* by Pamela Stephenson
4 *Buster's Diaries* by Roy Hattersley
5 *The Number Devil* by Hans Magnus Enzensberger
6 *A Short History of Nearly Everything* by Bill Bryson
7 *Portrait of a Killer* by Patricia Cornwell

Why the extracts have been selected

Extracts 1–3 give insights into the lives of public figures and show them in a sympathetic or entertaining way. Extract 3 tries to be more objective by exploring the subject's life from the standpoint of a psychologist.

Extracts 4–6 are all fun ways to explain difficult ideas and aim to make them easier to grasp.

The writer of Extract 7 is a crime novelist, writing about a real crime. To some extent she is writing as a fiction writer who has control over the story.

My Side
by *David Beckham*

This extract raises questions about why people write autobiographies. Like anyone with a high media profile, this writer has a great deal written about him in newspapers and magazines – not all of it accurate. The title of his autobiography *My Side* suggests that he wants to present his own version of events. As you read this extract you should focus on:

- how he uses information to create a particular image of himself
- whether this is an objective account or one manipulated to create an effect.

This extract is from the introduction to the book; it describes the press conference held to introduce the writer to Real Madrid, and an incident with a young supporter.

'Gracias, Senor Perez, Senor di Stefano, ladies and gentlemen…'

I left a split second for the translator to do his stuff. At first his microphone didn't seem to be working properly. I waited. And while I waited my mind went blank. Suddenly I was aware of the forest of cameras out in front of me, people around the hall craning heads in my direction. I'm glad I've learned to trust myself. I opened my mouth and the rest of it came.

'I have always loved football. Of course, I love my family…'

I looked down towards Victoria again: too right I love them.

'... and I have a wonderful life. But football is everything to me. To play for Real is a dream come true. Thank you to everyone for being here to share my arrival. Gracias.'

I held the shirt – my new shirt – up in front of me: 'Hola Madrid!'

The other directors of the club came over for the team photos and then Senor Perez led us offstage and back through the corridors to a room at the far end of the building, where there was a table laid out with tapas and biscuits and soft drinks. There's a room like this at every football club: a sloping ceiling and bench seats around the walls. They'd tidied this one up a bit, though. Then, I was taken through a door at the far end that led off into the changing rooms: not quite as imposing as the ones at the **Bernabeu** the day before.

I took my time pulling on the Real Madrid kit for the very first time. Then a couple of security guards and Simon and Jamie, from **SFX**, came through the changing room and we walked across to Numero 2, a training pitch with low stands on one side and at one end, both crammed with supporters. It took a moment for my eyes to adapt, stepping out into bright sunshine again. I ran through the gap in the fence and a couple of footballs were thrown towards me. I know I play for a living. Controlling a ball, keeping it up in the air, the odd trick: it's all second nature. But out on a patch of grass, in front of a couple of thousand supporters who are all thinking: show us? It felt a bit lonely out there, to be honest, even though the reception I got from the *madridistas* was all I could have hoped for: families everywhere, cheering and waving. I waved back. The photographers got their shots of David Beckham in a Real kit for the very first time.

Bernabeu Real Madrid's stadium
SFX a public relations company

How long was I going to be out here? What else did we need to do? I kicked a ball up into the crowd behind the goal. I peered up into the stand in front of me, trying to see who'd caught it, trying to get a clue as to how these same fans would take to me when we ran out at the Bernabeu, alongside the *Galacticos*, for a game. I knew I'd be back in Madrid to start work on 24 July. The whirl of the last 24 hours suddenly rushed to a full stop. The significance of what had happened today and the previous day swept over me, filled my chest like a blast of pure oxygen. It felt fantastic.

Suddenly, out of the corner of my eye, while the security guards followed my line of sight up into the crowd, I saw a figure away to my left, darting out from behind the frame of a floodlight pylon. A lad – eleven, twelve – tanned, black hair stood on end, bare chested and wearing a pair of jean shorts and some battered trainers. And he was haring towards me: I think I saw him before anyone else did. There were shouts of surprise from the crowd. The security people swivelled and looked towards me. Too late: the boy – named Alfonso, I found out later – was standing a couple of feet away from me. It was a shock but there wasn't anything about him to make me step back. His eyes were wide open, pleading, like he wanted something from me without knowing what. My instinct was to just hold my arms out towards him. He didn't need a second invitation: he jumped at me, laughing. I caught and held on, almost as tightly as he did. I waved away the security guys: this was just a boy who'd taken his chance. I managed to prise him off for long enough to motion over to Simon who was in front of the other stand:

'A shirt. I need another shirt.'

We walked across and met them halfway. I tried to give the shirt to him but Alfonso just stood in front of me,

Galacticos the Real Madrid team

tears in his eyes now. He raised his arms at either side. I dropped the shirt over his head. This was like some weird kind of ceremony going on here. I was half-aware that people around the ground were cheering and whistling. He pushed his arms through and the shirt settled on him, almost down to his knees. He looked up at me. His eyes were like a mirror: happiness, fear, awe, the wonder of the impossible having just happened. In a couple of hours' time, I would be on a plane back to England with my family. Time to start packing our bags. Where would Alfonso be then? I looked down into this boy's expectant, passionate face. I could see how hard he'd dreamt, how determined he'd been to be where he was now, standing there facing me. I felt like asking him; it felt like he was asking me:

'Who are you, son? Where did you come from? How did you come to be here?'

How Do You Want Me?
by *Ruby Wax*

In this extract the writer gives an entertaining and sometimes painful view of herself, made interesting by the use of humour and sharp observations. As you read this extract you should focus upon:

- how the writer has selected information about herself and her family in order to present herself in a particular way
- the ways in which she engages directly with the reader
- her use of humour to entertain.

As a successful actor and comedian, the writer gives every indication of being a larger-than-life character, full of energy and self-confidence. However, as her auto-biography shows, as a child she was often lonely, excluded by other children, and felt herself to be a misfit. In this extract, she considers why her childhood was so unusual and tries to explain how she became the adult she is.

My philosophy: who you are in the playground is exactly who you will be at the end of your life, unless something **cataclysmic** happens to you or you make a supreme effort to change your story. But it must be supreme. How are these parts cast? I don't know. All I know is that I just showed up one day at **recess**, was handed a script and assigned my character. Who cast me in this role? Was it in the stars or in the DNA? Or is there some natural selection going on like in the animal kingdom? How do they recognise head of the herd? The one with the longest

---

cataclysmic earth-shattering
recess (US) break

tusks? Who's the natural born joker in the cow pack? Which heifer is going to make Vegas?

So many questions.

For some reason I was not part of the common herd in the playground society and I do not know why I got exiled. Perhaps my parents sprayed me with weirdness dust. They clearly wore it, so maybe I picked it up. I had absolutely no chance to be one of the popular girls as they could smell I was not of their species; so I became one of the boys. I became their lackey, a 'runt/boy' who ran their dirty chores.

To trigger a memory of why I was rejected I tried to find some photos of me as a child. I noticed I had some drawbacks. Luckily my father chronicled every moment of my life in film and photographs, from potty training to summer camp – nothing was too embarrassing. Since I was an only child the spotlight was always trained on me. When I found the evidence, I saw immediately why everyone hated me.

I had front teeth that were so **protrusive** they were in another time zone – about an hour in front of my face. Kids thought my name was 'Roovy' since my lip flaps didn't meet. I made our dentist very rich from reining in the 'tusks'. He fitted me with a **sputnik-like** head brace that didn't so much bring my teeth to me but the rest of my body up to live under them. My first year in school I pretended to be a beaver. I took apart a Davy Crockett fur hat and pinned the tail on my bottom. This meant I couldn't hear the ridicule since I was far too busy sawing down trees and building dams.

My mother encouraged my unattractiveness by cutting my hair in a bowl shape, like a monk. She would also dress me in outfits to ensure I'd look older than her and uglier. Long before *The Sound of Music* I was in full

---

protrusive sticking out
sputnik-like like a space satellite

dirndl and **lederhosen**. From four years old on, I was dressed as an Alpinian sheep-herder while my mother was decked out in Yves Saint Laurent, Oscar de la Renta and Valentino couture.

You could hear the intake of breath as people realised such a bombshell had released something as plain as me. She always wore a mink coat or fox fur wrap where the head ate its own tail, smoking non-stop those extra long cigarettes. She was the beauty in the house, I didn't have a chance, I could only ever be understudy waiting for her demise. There she was, this golden goddess, nyloned legs soaring up from Italian, La Dolce Vita, high heels with leather ankle straps. I yearned for those legs and shoes; instead my feet were encased in saddle shoes, which she said I needed so I wouldn't develop bunions. (I did anyway to spite her. Ha ha). On shopping expeditions I'd scream for black patent leather pumps but they might have made me attractive so I never got them. Just hush puppies to keep me hushed. And I'd get, 'Come on Ruby, they're cute, believe me I'm your mother I would tell you. Sometimes, I'd sneak into her closet, which was off-limits, and see rows and rows of designer shoes lined up as if for an SS inspection.

Even as an infant things were strange. I know here in England, as children, you were read stories about Pooh Bear and his tiggily-wiggily friends. I was read German stories about Strange Peter who had twelve-inch nails and frizzed up hair like he had just been electrocuted. He would set fire to people for fun or cut off their thumbs for a laugh. Grimm's Fairy Takes was another bedtime favourite. I remember one charming character, Frau Rotzkauph (translation: snot-head) had a beard, a wart

---

dirndl a very full, old-fashioned skirt
lederhosen leather shorts
SS the Nazi special police

and ate her children. Then she proceeded to cook them in a pie for not washing their hands before eating. There was another tale about a goose that ate a whole family and how they had to be cut out of its carcass with an axe. They all jumped out smiling but covered in bile. I didn't need nightmares, they were read to me. It all makes perfect sense when you think that young Hitler must have gone to beddy-byes hearing those same enchanting little tales.

Even without this bedtime reading, I was somewhat **nihilistic**. I knew as an infant, when you lost your tooth, you were supposed to picture a beautiful fairy with wings and a wand who flew into your bedroom in the night to bring money just for you. By about five, I knew this was for a 'limited season' only and that later on I could have whole root canals and there'd be nothing under my pillow. And when I got older, it was clear that even if I had large vital organs removed she'd be a no-shower. I didn't believe in the tooth fairy, Santa, the Messiah, and certainly not Mr Wonderful; I knew nobody could save me.

Things were off-whack anyway, since I came from a German-speaking household, which caused me great embarrassment. You ordered food off the menu, it sounded like you were declaring war in Europe: 'I'll have the schvenkacktenzinka schvinetang Ga retchkavkch...' People came out of the kitchen with their hands up.

---

nihilistic rejecting accepted beliefs and preferring to believe in nothing

Billy
by *Pamela Stephenson*

This extract is from the comedian Billy Connolly's biography, written by his wife. She raises some interesting issues about the difficulty of writing about celebrities accurately and honestly. She suggests that there is no such thing as the absolute truth, there is only one person's version of it. As you read this extract you should focus upon:

- whether the writer is presenting the truth or only part of it
- how she shows the ways in which past experiences influence what we become
- how she uses description to build up a realistic picture of the place.

This extract is about the slum tenement building in Glasgow where Billy Connolly grew up, and the lasting effect that this has had on his life.

Ironically, Billy's very earliest memory is one of being terrified by a circle of light. Until he was three years old, he and his beloved sister Florence slept in a curtained-off alcove in the kitchen. One evening she aimed a mirror reflection onto the wall, allowing it to pirouette and chase him until he screamed for mercy.

He had been born right next to that alcove on the kitchen floor, all eleven pounds of him plopping out onto freezing linoleum. The rage that followed this unceremonious introduction to the world has never left him, although it was a **serendipitous** launching for a future enemy of the **bourgeoisie**. For eight months he

---

serendipitous something fortunate that happens by chance
bourgeoisie the middle classes

nestled in a wooden drawer with not one Fisher-Price contraption in sight.

His family's living arrangements were similar to those of thousands of other inhabitants of Glasgow, a city that had come to be defined by row upon row of late-nineteenth-century apartment buildings known as 'the tenements'. Those fine architectural soldiers had originally been created by Glasgow's Improvement Trust, as model housing for working-class families. But by the time the Connollys moved into half of the third floor of 65 Dover Street in Anderston, many of them had deteriorated into rotting slums that would need more than a spot of paint to 'take the bad look off them', as Billy would say.

The classically derived elevations in red or yellow sandstone were usually pleasant enough, but the interiors were thoroughly depressing. A dingy central staircase, stinking of cabbage and cats, spiralled upwards to the flats. Two or more poky apartments were squeezed into each floor, usually with just two rooms apiece, and a communal lavatory out on the landing. Some families were lumbered with the 'coffin end', or corner apartment, which was even smaller than the rest.

The buildings themselves butted right onto the street and were usually entered via an interior alleyway known as a close. The 'Wally' closes, as some were called, were beautifully tiled halfway up the wall, with a leafy motif running along the top. Such finery, however, ended abruptly at the threshold of a darker, often treacherous, tunnel known as the 'dunny' (short for dungeon), that dead-ended in an enclosed rear courtyard, itself a veritable assault-course of broken bicycles, flapping knickers, and **reeking middens**.

Considering it now through a haze of nostalgia, Billy says the Glasgow tenement is a New York **brownstone** without a fire escape. Some of the buildings certainly had grandeur and, like their New York counterparts, are now sought after by the well-to-do. Billy's first home was not one of those. The Dover Street flat had only two rooms: a kitchen-living room, with a niche where the children slept, and another room for their parents. The entire family bathed in the kitchen sink and there was no hot water at all. As an enduring legacy of his early cramped existence, Billy is now quite uncomfortable in large living spaces. He sighs over the phone to me from fabulous hotels all over the world: 'They've gone and upgraded me again. Bloody Presidential Suite this time.'

I let him off lightly, because I know it's a genuine problem for him. Others who achieve renown cannot wait to sprawl sideways on a California King four-poster with a big-screen TV in every corner and a whirlpool on the deck, but not Billy. He has never really liked our Los Angeles house because of its unfamiliar spaciousness, and prefers to hide out in his tiny study for hours on end, drinking gallons of tea and plunking on his banjo.

---

reeking middens stinking piles of rubbish
brownstone old houses, once poor, now fashionable

Buster's Diaries
by *Roy Hattersley*

In these diary entries the writer takes on the persona of a dog and imagines all the misunderstandings and confusions that a dog might experience about some of the more absurd aspects of human life. The writer (or his dog, Buster) relates in a humorous way events that have appeared in the news. As you read these diary entries you should focus upon:

- how the writer creates humour by writing as if he is a dog
- how the writer uses the viewpoint of a dog to show how ridiculous humans can be
- how the writer manipulates sentence construction to create a comic effect.

The writer is a well-known politician. He is also the owner of a dog called Buster.

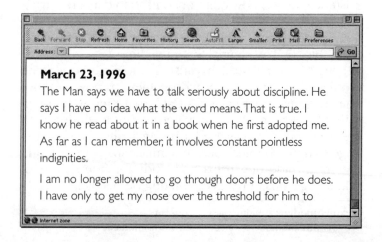

March 23, 1996

The Man says we have to talk seriously about discipline. He says I have no idea what the word means. That is true. I know he read about it in a book when he first adopted me. As far as I can remember, it involves constant pointless indignities.

I am no longer allowed to go through doors before he does. I have only to get my nose over the threshold for him to

shout, 'Back up! Back up!' I am then expected to walk backwards and stand absolutely still until he goes out in front of me. He has decided to prove that he is senior to me in the pack. It is obvious to me that he isn't. If he were leader, instead of all this 'Back up!' and 'Sit!' nonsense, he would just bite me when I annoy him.

April 6, 1996

There has been an incident. The newspapers said it took place in the park, but my behaviour in the park was perfectly normal. The extraordinary event happened in the street when we were on our way home from the morning's walk. A police car pulled up alongside us. Two police officers got out, one of each sort. The policeman spoke. 'Excuse me, Sir. Has your dog killed a goose in St James's Park?' he asked. 'Not that I know of,' the Man replied, looking startled.

The policewoman patted me on the side of the head in the way that the RSPCA recommend for greeting strange dogs. She held up her hand as if she were stopping traffic. It had blood on it. 'Good God,' the Man said. Then the policewoman ran her finger round the inside of my collar. A lot of feathers came out. The police officer told the Man, 'Get in the car.' The Man got in the front seat. I jumped on his knee and, since I was facing him, I licked his face. He said, 'For God's sake, not now Buster.' The policeman said, 'You are not obliged to say anything, but if you fail to mention anything that you subsequently use in evidence ...' When we got home, the Man said, 'You've really done it this time, Buster.'

The police say I broke the law by being off the lead in the

park. It is not true. I had not been off the lead. But the Man had. He was bending down doing his usual peculiar business with the plastic bag, when I gave the expanding lead a big tug. He let go. So I trotted off, and ended up in the rhododendron bushes, with the lead trailing behind me. For several minutes, he was totally out of my control and in breach of the park's regulations.

I was not alone in the rhododendron bushes for long. Suddenly a goose appeared. Geese are supposed to be frightened by dogs and fly away. But this one barely seemed to notice that I was there. It just fluttered its wings a bit and went on pecking at the ground. Naturally I was offended. So I gave it a nip in the back of the neck. It waddled off and I went into my stalking mode. When it flopped over the fence between the path and the pond, I lost interest. How was I to know that it belonged to the Queen?

April 9, 1996

The newspapers found out about the goose. The Man thinks a gardener was given a biscuit for telling them. This morning there were photographers waiting for us when we went for our walk. We sat on a park bench whilst they took our picture. I was the star, gazing up at him like Man's Best Friend and licking his face. The *Evening Standard* had a billboard, 'Park Murder Suspect: First Pictures'.

Most of the reports were lies. Some said I had bitten the goose's head off. Others said it lay eviscerated on the path. The Man explained that the newspapers had to invent better stories than the truth – a little nip isn't news, but horrible

mutilation is. And I'm supposed to be the one with the wolf inside me!

I have become very famous. This morning people stopped us in the street and told him not to thrash me or have me shot. Dog owners sent bones through the post. There were cartoons in the *Guardian* and the *Daily Telegraph*. A Dachsund called Lottie telephoned to propose marriage. He wrote back to say I was too young. People we did not know made jokes. The Man got bored with the jokes very quickly – particularly 'Has he killed a goose today?' and 'Still catching your supper, is he?' I loved them. We met the police officer in the street and he said he was sure we would hear no more about the dead goose. He was wrong.

April 12, 1996

I am getting letters from all over the country. Some are from humans pretending to be dogs and some are from humans admitting to be humans. The letters which are signed by dogs all say that I was right and the goose was wrong. The letters which are signed by humans all tell the Man that he must be kind to me and not have me shot.

The Man is going to reply to everyone. He has written one letter for the dogs and another for the humans and has spent all afternoon trying to decide who should get which letter. As soon as he had posted the first batch, he realised he had made a terrible mistake. Lulu is a House of Commons secretary not a Pekinese. I think Countess Beatrice de Villiers of Compton Basset is probably a pedigree German Shepherd dog and not an English aristocrat.

The Number Devil
by *Hans Magnus Enzensberger*

This extract combines the conventions of a traditional fairy story with the explanation of complex but fascinating mathematical ideas. As you read this extract, you should focus upon:
- the features of story writing
- other ways in which the writer appeals to children
- how the writer breaks down information to help the reader understand difficult ideas
- how the writer shares his enthusiasm for his subject matter.

Robert is a boy who finds numbers tricky. The number devil visits him in his dreams to help him overcome his fear of mathematics.

'Well,' said the number devil, puffing himself up again, 'I'm only doing it for you! You're the one who's afraid of numbers. You're the one who wants everything simple so you won't get mixed up.'

'But all those ones get so boring after a while. I don't think it's simple. It's just that all those ones give me a headache. They actually make things more complicated than they are.'

'Well, well,' said the number devil, clearing the sky with a casual wave of the hand. 'So you agree we need something less clumsy than 1 + 1 + 1 + 1 ... Numbers, for instance. Which is why I invented them.'

'You? You expect me to believe that you invented numbers?'

'Me or a few others. It doesn't matter who exactly. Why are you so suspicious? What do you say I show you how to make all numbers out of ones?'

'Okay. How?'

'Simple. I start as follows:
1 x 1 = 1

And go on to:
11 x 11

I bet you need your calculator for that.'

'Don't be silly,' said Robert.
'11 x 11 = 121'

'See?' said the number devil. 'You've made a two out of nothing but ones. Now try this:
111 x 111'

'That's too hard. I can't do it in my head.'

'Then use your calculator.'

'My calculator! You don't think I take it to bed with me, do you?'

'Then use this one,' he said, pressing one into Robert's hand. It had a funny feel to it, slimy, like dough, and it was a sickly shade of green, but it worked. Robert entered: 111 x 111
and got:
12321

'Cool,' said Robert. 'Now we have a three.'

'Right. Just keep going.'

So Robert entered the following:
1111 x 1111 = 1234321
11111 x 11111 = 123454321

'Very good,' said the number devil, patting Robert on the shoulder. 'I'm sure you've noticed that not only do you get a new number each time, you get a number that reads the same forwards and backwards, like ANNA or TOOT or ROTATOR.'

Robert thought that this was a pretty good trick, and so he tried six ones as well - and it worked! But when he got to
1111111 x 1111111
the calculator gave up the ghost. To Robert's surprise, it suddenly went *Pfft!* And melted down into a sickly green goo.

'Yuck!' said Robert, wiping the green mess from his fingers.

'All you need is a bigger calculator or a computer. A computer would spit out the answer in no time.'

'Are you sure?'

'Of course I'm sure.'

Robert thought that the number devil was a bit too confident. Maybe he was just bluffing. Robert decided to take a chance and said, 'You haven't tried it with
11 111 111 111 x 11 111 111 111
have you?'

'No, can't say I have.'

'Well, I bet it doesn't work.'

The number devil started doing the problem in his head, but his face turned bright red again and swelled up like a balloon. Was it because he was angry, Robert wondered, or because the problem was hard?

'Wait a second,' the number devil mumbled. 'I can't seem to come up with anything. Damnation! You were right. It doesn't work. How did you know?'

'I didn't. You don't think I'm crazy enough to try a problem like that do you? I was just guessing.'

'Guessing? Guessing is not allowed in mathematics! Mathematics is an exact science!'

'But when you said that numbers don't stop, that they go on till the cows come home, that was a guess, wasn't it?'

'How dare you? What are you, anyway? A beginner! A rank amateur! And you want to teach me my trade?'

He grew bigger and fatter with every word; he started huffing and puffing. Robert was frightened.

'You pinhead! You pip-squeak! You stuck-up little number midget!' he screamed, and no sooner had the number devil got the last word out than he burst with a great big bang.

Robert woke up. He had fallen out of bed and was a little dizzy, but he laughed to think he had outwitted the number devil.

A Short History of Nearly Everything

by *Bill Bryson*

In this extract, the writer presents difficult material in an accessible and entertaining way. As you read this extract you should focus upon:
- how the writer chooses informal and enthusiastic language to make the information appear less threatening
- the writer's concern to interest the reader in the character behind the story.

The writer is trying to make boring or difficult subjects more interesting and easier to understand. In this extract, he is writing about Isaac Newton, the famous scientist. Newton's most famous work, Mathematical Principles of Natural Philosophy *(or* Principia*) is important, but is also difficult to understand.*

Once in a great while, a few times in history, a human mind produces an observation so acute and unexpected that people can't quite decide which is more amazing – the fact or the thinking of it. The appearance of the *Principia* was one of those moments. It made Newton instantly famous. For the rest of his life he would be draped with **plaudits** and honours, becoming, among much else, the first person in Britain knighted for scientific achievement. Even the great German mathematician Gottfried von Leibniz, with whom Newton had a long, bitter fight over priority for the invention of the calculus, thought his contributions to mathematics equal to all the accumulated work that had

plaudits praise

preceded him. 'Nearer the gods no mortal may approach,' wrote **Halley** in a sentiment that was endlessly echoed by his contemporaries and by many others since.

Although the *Principia* has been called 'one of the most inaccessible books ever written' (Newton intentionally made it difficult so that he wouldn't be pestered by mathematical 'smatterers', as he called them), it was a beacon to those who could follow it. It not only explained mathematically the orbits of heavenly bodies, but also identified the attractive force that got them moving in the first place – gravity. Suddenly every motion in the universe made sense.

At the *Principia's* heart were Newton's three laws of motion (which state, very **baldly**, that a thing moves in the direction in which it is pushed; that it will keep moving in a straight line until some other force acts to slow or deflect it; and that every action has an opposite and equal reaction) and his universal law of gravitation. This states that every object in the universe exerts a tug on every other. It may not seem like it, but as you sit here now you are pulling everything around you – walls, ceiling, lamp, pet cat – towards you with your own little (indeed, very little) gravitational field. And these things are also pulling on you. It was Newton who realised that the pull of any two objects is, to quote **Feynman** again, 'proportional to the mass of each and varies inversely as the square of the distance between them'. Put another way, if you double the distance between two objects, the attraction between them becomes four times weaker. This can be expressed with the formula

$$F = G \; \frac{mm'}{r^2}$$

Halley Edmond Halley (1656–1742) English astronomer and mathematician
baldly simply
Feynman Richard Feynmann (1918–88) American physicist

which is of course way beyond anything that most of us could make practical use of, but at least we can appreciate that it is elegantly compact. A couple of brief multiplications, a simple division and, bingo, you know your gravitational position wherever you go. It was the first really universal law of nature ever **propounded** by a human mind, which is why Newton is everywhere regarded with such profound esteem.

The *Principia*'s production was not without drama. To Halley's horror, just as work was nearing completion Newton and **Hooke** fell into dispute over the priority for the inverse square law and Newton refused to release the crucial third volume, without which the first two made little sense. Only with some frantic **shuttle diplomacy** and the most liberal applications of flattery did Halley manage finally to extract the concluding volume from the **erratic** professor.

Halley's traumas were not yet quite over. The Royal Society had promised to publish the work, but now pulled out, citing financial embarrassment. The year before, the Society had backed a costly flop called *The History of Fishes*, and suspected that the market for a book on mathematical principles would be less than **clamorous**. Halley, whose means were not great, paid for the book's publication out of his own pocket. Newton, as was his custom, contributed nothing. To make matters worse, Halley at this time had just accepted a position as the society's clerk, and he was informed that the society could no longer afford to provide him with a promised salary of £50 per annum. He was to be paid instead in copies of *The History of Fishes*.

---

propounded put forward for others to consider
Hooke Robert Hooke (1635–1703) English scientist
shuttle diplomacy negotiations carried out by one person between two other people who are not on speaking terms with one another
erratic unpredictable
clamorous strongly expressed

Portrait of a Killer
by *Patricia Cornwell*

This extract comes from a book that claims to tell the truth about famous crimes. However, the story has many features in common with crime fiction. As you read this extract, you should focus upon:
- how the writer uses the patterns, structures and language of fiction to create impact
- whether the writer is more interested in creating a good story that satisfies the reader by giving a solution to the puzzle, or revealing the truth with all the questions that remain to be answered.

The writer is a well-known writer of crime fiction, but in Portrait of a Killer *she turns her attention to a real crime: the five murders committed in 1888 by the person who came to be known as Jack the Ripper. She claims to have identified this serial killer as Walter Richard Sickert, an artist, and her book tells the story of how, she alleges, he carried out the crimes.*

Monday, August 6, 1888, was a Bank Holiday in London. The city was a carnival of wondrous things to do for as little as pennies if one could spare a few.

The bells of Windsor's Parish Church and St George's Chapel rang throughout the day. Ships were dressed in flags, and royal salutes boomed from cannons to celebrate the Duke of Edinburgh's forty-fourth birthday.

The Crystal Palace offered a dazzling spectrum of special programmes: organ recitals, military band concerts, a 'monster display of fireworks,' a grand fairy ballet, ventriloquists, and 'world famous minstrel performances.' Madam Tussaud's featured a special wax model of Frederick II lying in state and, of course, the ever-popular Chamber of Horrors. Other delicious horrors awaited whose who could afford theatre tickets and were in the mood for a morality play or just a good old-fashioned fright. *Dr Jekyll and Mr Hyde* was playing to sold-out houses. The famous American actor Richard Mansfield was brilliant as Jekyll and Hyde at Henry Irving's Lyceum, and the Opera Comique had its version, too, although poorly reviewed and in the midst of a scandal because the theatre had adapted Robert Louis Stevenson's novel without permission.

On this Bank Holiday there were horse and cattle shows; special 'cheap rates' on trains; and the bazaars in Covent Garden overflowing with Sheffield plates, gold, jewellery, used military uniforms. If one wanted to pretend to be a soldier on this relaxed but rowdy day, he could do so with little expense and no questions asked. Or one could impersonate a copper by renting an authentic Metropolitan Police uniform from Angel's Theatrical Costumes in Camden Town, scarcely a two-mile stroll from where the handsome Walter Richard Sickert lived.

Twenty-eight-year-old Sickert had given up his obscure acting career for the higher calling of art. He was a painter, an etcher, a student of James McNeill Whistler, and a disciple of Edgar Degas. Young Sickert was himself a work of art: slender, with a strong upper body from swimming, a perfectly angled nose and jaw, thick blond hair, and blue eyes that were as **inscrutable** and penetrating as his secret thoughts and piercing mind. One might almost have called him pretty, except for his mouth, which could narrow into a hard, cruel line. His precise height is unknown, but a friend of his described him as a little above average. Photographs and several

---

inscrutable impossible to understand

items of clothing donated to the Tate Gallery Archive in the 1980s suggest he was probably five foot eight or nine.

Sickert was fluent in German, English, French, and Italian. He knew Latin well enough to teach it to friends, and he was well acquainted with Danish and Greek and possibly knew a smattering of Spanish and Portuguese. He was said to read the classics in their original languages, but he didn't always finish a book once he started it. It wasn't uncommon to find dozens of novels strewn about, opened to the last page that had snagged his interest. Mostly, Sickert was addicted to newspapers, magazines, and journals.

Until his death in 1942, his studios and studies looked like a recycling centre for just about every bit of newsprint to roll off the European presses. One might ask how any hard-working person could find the time to go through four, five, six, ten newspapers a day, but Sickert had a method. He didn't bother with what didn't interest him, whether it was politics, economics, world affairs, wars, or people. Nothing mattered to Sickert unless it somehow affected Sickert.

He usually preferred to read about the latest entertainment to come to town, to scrutinise art critiques, to turn quickly to any story about crime, and to search for his own name if there was any reason it might be in print on a given day. He was fond of letters to the editor, especially ones he wrote and signed with a pseudonym. Sickert relished knowing what other people were doing, especially in the privacy of their own not-always-so-tidy Victorian lives. 'Write, write, write!' he would beg his friends. 'Tell me in detail all *sorts* of things, things that have amused you and *how* and *when* and *where*, and all sorts of gossip about every one.'

Sickert despised the upper class, but he was a star stalker. He somehow managed to hobnob with the major celebrities of the day: Henry Irving and Ellen Terry,

Aubrey Beardsley, Henry James, Max Beerbohm, Oscar Wilde, Monet, Renoir, Pissarro, Rodin, André Gide, Édouard Dujardin, Proust, Members of Parliament. But he did not necessarily know many of them, and no one – famous or otherwise – ever really knew him. Not even his first wife, Ellen, who would turn forty in less than two weeks. Sickert may not have given much thought to his wife's birthday on this Bank Holiday, but it was extremely unlikely he had forgotten it.

He was much admired for his amazing memory. Throughout his life he would amuse dinner guests by performing long passages of musicals and plays, dressed for the parts, his recitations flawless. Sickert would not have forgotten that Ellen's birthday was August 18th and a very easy occasion to ruin. Maybe he would 'forget.' Maybe he would vanish into one of his secret rented hovels that he called studios. Maybe he would take Ellen to a romantic café in Soho and leave her alone at the table while he dashed off to a music hall and then stayed out the rest of the night. Ellen loved Sickert all her sad life, despite his cold heart, his pathological lying, his self-centredness, and his habit of disappearing for days – even weeks – without warning or explanation.

Walter Sickert was an actor by nature more than by virtue of employment. He lived on the centre stage of his secret, fantasy-driven life and was just as comfortable moving about unnoticed in the deep shadows of isolated streets as he was in the midst of throbbing crowds. He had a great range of voice and was a master of greasepaint and wardrobe. So gifted at disguise was he that as a boy he often went about unrecognised by his neighbours and family.

Throughout his long and celebrated life, he was notorious for constantly changing his appearance with a variety of beards and moustaches, for his bizarre dress that in some cases constituted costumes, for his hairstyles

– including shaving his head. He was, wrote French artist and friend Jacques-Emile Blanche, a '**Proteus**.' Sickert's 'genius for camouflage in dress, in the fashion of wearing his hair, and in his manner of speaking rival **Fregoli**'s,' Blanche recalled. In a portrait Wilson Steer painted of Sickert in 1890, Sickert sports a phony-looking moustache that resembles a squirrel's tail pasted above his mouth.

He also had a penchant for changing his name. His acting career, paintings, etchings, drawings, and prolific letters to colleagues, friends, and newspapers reveal many personas: Mr Nemo (Latin for 'Mr Nobody'), An Enthusiast, A Whistlerite, Walter R. Sickert, Richard Sickert, W.R. Sickert, W.S., R.S., S., Dick, W. St., Rd. Sickert LL.D., R.St.W., R.St.A.R.A., and RDSt A.R.A.

Proteus in Greek mythology, the son of a sea god who could change his shape as he pleased
Fregoli Leopold Fregoli, an Italian mimic and magician

Activities

My Side

1 It was particularly important for the writer to show that he was happy to be in Spain and playing for Real Madrid. Can you find two ways in the first six paragraphs in which he does this?

2 The writer mentions that Simon and Jamie from SFX are with him. SFX is a public relations company that helps to create public images for celebrities. Imagine you are interviewing Jamie about the image he wants to convey of David and Victoria Beckham at this press conference. In pairs, work out **four** questions you could ask and write his reply in the form of a script. Below are two questions to start you off.

Interviewer: What advice did you give David before he spoke?

Jamie: ....

Interviewer: Why was it important for Victoria to be at the welcome meeting?

Jamie: ....

3 Imagine that you are able to observe the writer during the events that he describes here. Try to put aside any ideas you might already have about him and note down your impressions from what you see and hear. Work in pairs to collect ideas and evidence on a chart like the one below.

My impressions	The evidence
At first he is nervous and uncertain, but becomes more confident.	He hesitates and seems to have forgotten what he wants to say.
His family is very important to him.	

4 Re-read the last section of this account starting *Suddenly out of the corner of my eye…* In pairs, discuss the questions below, then share your ideas with the class.

- Why do you think the writer uses so much detail to describe the boy?
- Why does he include this incident?
- Why does he choose to finish with those three questions?
- Do you think this incident really happened in the way the writer describes it?

5 Use the notes you made for Activity 3 and your ideas from Activity 4 to write about what impression this extract gives you of the writer. Do you think what he has presented about himself is the truth?

How Do You Want Me?

1 Why does the writer ask so many questions in the first paragraph? Can you sum them up as just one question?

2 Like many of us, rather than risk rejection, the writer simply didn't compete with the other girls. What did she do instead? How does her description make her seem smaller and less significant?

3 As we might expect, the writer uses humour to entertain us, but at the same time she makes some serious points.

   a Find **three** examples of how she uses exaggeration to create humour.

   b Find **three** examples of how she uses visual humour (the creation of funny images or pictures).

   c Find **one** example of how she includes things that might seem odd or unexpected.

4 The writer suggests that her relationship with her mother was not good. What examples can you find that show this? How would you describe this relationship?

5 What reasons are there to feel sorry for the writer as a child? You could think about:

- her appearance and the clothes she had to wear
- how she fitted in at school
- how she was treated by her mother
- how her experience of growing up and family life were different from other children.

Do you get the impression that the writer feels sorry for herself?

6 How much do you trust this extract to be telling you the truth? Is there anything here that you think she might have made up? Do you think she has changed anything in order to entertain her readers?

7 What do you find interesting about the way the writer presents herself in her autobiography? In your answer you could include all or some of the following:

- the way she uses different sorts of humour
- her description of family relationships
- whether you feel sorry for her or not
- how honest you think she has been.

Billy

1 In the section just before this extract, the writer describes a time when the adult Billy had been struck with stage fright, but had overcome his fear and stepped out into the spotlight. How does the opening of this extract make a connection with that event?

2 Since Billy himself could not have told the writer about his birth, who do you think supplied this information? Do you think it is true?

3 The writer tells us that the outside of the apartment building or 'tenement' where Billy grew up seemed quite attractive, but that inside, it was very different. Copy the table below and list the positive and negative phrases she uses to describe 65 Dover Street.

Negative description	Positive description
• rotting slums	• model housing

In your own words, describe the place where Billy Connolly lived as a child. Does this seem like a good place to be brought up in?

4 How has the passage of time affected Billy's ideas and memories about where he grew up? Look in paragraph 6 for a phrase that describes his attitude now.

5 The writer is interested in how people's early experiences affect them in later life. What does she tell us has been the long-term effect on Billy of growing up in this cramped environment?

6 Billy Connolly is now a very successful and wealthy entertainer. In pairs, make a list of things in this extract that surprise you about his background. Is there anything you find difficult to believe? If so, why?

7 Think about your own experience of growing up. What events, people or places do you think will have a lasting effect on you? Why are they so important? What did you learn from them and how have they made a difference to you?

Buster's Diaries

1 The writer deliberately views events from an unusual viewpoint. Explore how he does this by completing the following tasks.

a Much of the humour in the extract is created by Buster's failure to understand the differences in acceptable behaviour for humans and dogs. Find **three** examples of this from the diary entries.

b Explain why the following quotation is amusing: *The police say I broke the law by being off the lead in the park. It is not true. I had not been off the lead. But the Man had.*

c Look at the last paragraph of the entry for 6 April and explain how the writer makes it seem that the goose was responsible for its own death and that Buster was blameless.

d Remind yourself of the differences between simple, compound and complex sentences.

- **simple**   a single clause or unit of sense, for example: *It is not true*

- **compound** two or more clauses of equal weight, joined by a conjunction (e.g. *and*, *or*, *but*), for example: *It just fluttered its wings a bit **and** went on pecking the ground*

- **complex**   a main clause (MC) with one or more subordinate or dependent clauses (SC), for example: SC When it flopped over the fence between the path and the pond, MC I lost interest.

Read the final two paragraphs of the entry for 6 April. One sort of sentence is used much more than others. Which one is it? Why are there so many more of these?

e Look at the second paragraph in the entry for 9 April. This is the only paragraph that uses words like *eviscerated* and *horribly mutilated*. Write down what these words mean, then say why this type of language is appropriate in this passage.

2 Imagine that you are either a Rottweiller or a toy poodle. Write a letter to Buster, ensuring that your assumed personality is made clear through your writing. Think about the ways in which the writer (and Buster) create humour and try them out for yourself.

The Number Devil

1 The writer uses many language features of children's story writing in this information text. Explore how he does it by completing the tasks below.

   a In order to tell the story, the writer has had to create characters for the number devil and Robert. Sort the list below into two columns, one for the number devil and one for Robert.

- dignified
- proud
- intelligent
- modern
- old-fashioned
- superior
- sceptical
- confident
- lacking in confidence
- suspicious
- down to earth
- ordinary
- extraordinary
- kind
- avuncular (like a kindly uncle)
- hot-tempered
- cheeky

   b Select **two** of the characteristics you have chosen for the number devil and Robert and find quotations to support your choices.

c As well as creating characters, dialogue is also a useful
way of breaking the explanation into steps. Pick out the
piece of dialogue where the number devil makes it clear
to Robert what he should have noticed about the
numbers.

d What does the writer say about the number devil's
calculator to make it fit into a story involving magic?

e What makes the ending of this story so satisfying?

2 What do you find interesting about the way in which the writer
has presented this explanation of a complex mathematical
idea? You could include all or some the following:

- how the writer created the characters of the number
devil and Robert
- the use of dramatic, exciting language
- the use of dialogue
- the use of creatures such as devils, that are more usually
associated with fairy stories than with mathematics
- the use of a satisfying traditional story ending.

A Short History of Nearly Everything

1 The writer uses informal language and enthusiastic
vocabulary to make us feel that the information is not too
difficult to understand. He also gives us a few bits of
information to give us some insight into Newton's
character and to gain our interest. Explore how he does
this by completing the tasks below.

a List the words and phrases from the first paragraph that
suggest that Newton's discovery was important and
exciting.

b One way in which the writer makes the subject
interesting is by making us think about Newton the
person as well as about the things that he wrote. Write
a short character study of Newton. Support your choice
of characteristics with examples/quotations from the
text. You could start your writing like this: *Newton was*

a great mathematician. He was recognised and respected by his competitors. Bryson says that the German mathematician Gottfried von Liebniz admitted that Newton's work was 'equal to all the accumulated work that had preceded him'. This is high praise, as...

c One way in which the writer helps to make the subject appear less threatening is by using informal language and sentence structures. Write a paragraph about how accessible the language is. Comment on and provide examples of the following:

- informal/colloquial (casual, conversational) language
- informal sentence structures, particularly the use of dashes
- writing in the second person ('you').

2 You have been asked to produce a set of revision cards for students' science tests. Design a card reminding students of Newton's three laws of motion. Work to the following specification:

- A5-sized cards
- title, bold and underlined, at the top
- information in bullet points
- up to 75 words of text
- up to three clear, simple diagrams.

Like Bill Bryson, you should aim to inform and explain in an accessible way.

Portrait of a Killer

1 The writer uses her fiction-writing skills to create a gripping argument that Walter Sickert was Jack the Ripper. Explore how she does this by completing the tasks below.

a Read the first four paragraphs of the extract carefully. Write about how the writer creates the impression of a lively, bustling London on August Bank Holiday Monday in 1888. Comment on at least three uses of lively language, saying why they are effective. Also note how the writer uses lists and quotations.

b The description of London must be a mixture of the writer's imagination and historical fact. Select **four** pieces of factual information from the first four paragraphs. Comment on why the writer makes deliberate use of this material from her research.

c Look particularly at the fourth paragraph and explain how the writer begins to make the reader think that it would be possible for Sickert to pass himself off as someone else.

d The fifth paragraph gives us a largely factual description of Sickert, but some of the writer's words allow us to pick up on her feelings about this man. Choose the quotation that best shows this.

e This extract comes from the beginning of Cornwell's book, in which she builds up a story accusing Sickert of being Jack the Ripper. How many hints can you find in the extract to suggest that, in her view, Sickert is not to be trusted?

2 Choose a character from a television soap opera. Write two or three paragraphs describing that character and his or her surroundings. Aim to grip the reader, using some of the fiction-writing techniques explored in Activity 1.

Comparing the extracts

All the extracts in this section pose questions about whether or not they are really literary, really non-fiction or are telling the whole truth. The activities below ask you to draw some comparisons between the texts in terms of:

- the purpose of the writing
- the audience for the writing
- the way the writing is crafted according to purpose and audience
- the impact and significance the writing has on you as a reader.

The final discussion activity asks you to make some judgements about the qualities of each of the extracts in this section and come to some conclusions about whether they are literary non-fiction.

1 Look again at the two extracts that explain difficult ideas in entertaining ways: *The Number Devil* and *A Short History of Nearly Everything. The Number Devil* is written as a children's story and *A Short History of Nearly Everything* sounds informal and conversational.

    a Make a list of the features of each kind of text.

    b **Either** write about the idea of all numbers being made from the number 1 in an informal, conversational way **or** write about Newton's three laws of motion as a children's story.

2 Having read all the extracts in this section, arrange them in order according to how much you trust the author to tell the truth. The one you feel is the most truthful should go at the top and the one you feel is the least truthful should go at the bottom. Consider the passage that comes last on your list; why do you trust this author least? Give at least **three** reasons supported by evidence from the text.

3 Below is a list of qualities we might expect to find in a good piece of autobiographical writing:

- it should tell you more than just facts about the person
- it should convince you that it is a true reflection of the person
- it should make you feel that the person has understood themselves and can express difficult ideas clearly
- it should be written in a way that makes you feel as if the writer is sharing their thoughts with you.

Look again at the two pieces of autobiographical writing in this section, those by Ruby Wax and David Beckham. Working in pairs, take each of the bullet points above and say whether you think it is true for each extract. You need to be able to give reasons for your opinions.

4 In working through these extracts you have explored a range of features that make them interesting or distinctive. All of the texts are about things that have really happened, so they all belong with non-fiction rather than fiction. However, the crucial question is, are they *literary* non-fiction?

In small groups, working on a copy of the grid on page 199, review each of the texts and decide which of the criteria for literary non-fiction each one meets. Then decide which extracts are definitely literary non-fiction and which ones you are less confident about. Be prepared to share your judgements. Remember that there are no right and wrong answers!

Criteria grid for literary and non-fiction texts

Criteria	Text 1	Text 2	Text 3	Text 4	Text 5	Text 6	Text 7	Text 8
Does it explore ideas rather than just present facts?								
Has the writer deliberately crafted the writing to make a difference to the feelings of the reader?								
Does it use language in lively and imaginative ways?								
Has attention been paid to the sounds of words and the rhythms of sentences?								
Does it use the patterns and structures of fiction writing to create impact, for example, to create tension?								
Is it written to last and not just perform a short-lived job or function?								

Routes through the collection

The following grids may be used to group extracts according to particular teaching points that the teacher wishes to make, e.g. *writing to create humour.*

Text type, purpose and level of challenge for each text

	Text type	Purpose	Pre-1914	Other cultures	Level of challenge
Section 1 Viewpoints: seeing people and places through a writer's eyes					
Spaghetti Bolognese	Autobiography (extract). 1st, present	Entertain and reflect			Easily accessible
Cider with Rosie	Autobiography (extract). 1st, past	Entertain and reflect			Easily accessible
Bad Blood	Autobiography (extract). 1st, past	Explore character and reflect			Moderately challenging
My Place – Wolverhampton	Essay (whole text). 1st, present into past	Inform and persuade			Moderately challenging
Remembering Aunt Marie	Autobiographical short story (whole text). 1st, past	Entertain and reflect		✓	Easily accessible
The Tiger Ladies	Memoir (extract). 1st, present	Record and reflect		✓	Moderately challenging

	Text type	Purpose	Pre-1914	Other cultures	Level of challenge
Wild Swans	Historical autobiography (extract). 1st, past	Record and reflect		✓	Moderately challenging
A Middle Eastern Affair	Personal recollection (extract). 1st, present into past	Describe and reflect		✓	Challenging
Section 2 Dramatic moments: experiencing the feelings of a writer					
In Black and White	Historical biography (extract). 3rd, past	Record and inform		✓	Moderately challenging
The Cruellest Miles	Real-life adventure (extract). 3rd, past	Entertain and inform			Moderately challenging
Amy Johnson, Queen of the Air	Biography (extract). 3rd, past	Entertain and inform			Moderately challenging
Terra Incognita	Travel writing (extract). 3rd, past	Reflect on historical events			Challenging
A Covered Wagon Girl	Diary (extract). 1st, past	Personal account and record	✓	✓	Easily accessible
Don't Let's Go to the Dogs Tonight	Autobiography (extract). 1st, present	Record and reflect		✓	Moderately challenging
Section 3 Observation: involvement in a writer's thoughts and memories					
Christmas at school	Autobiography (extract). 1st, past	Entertain			Easily accessible
My East End	Historical account (extract). 1st, past	Record and reflect			Easily accessible

	Text type	Purpose	Pre-1914	Other cultures	Level of challenge
Profiting from Child's Play	Newspaper article (whole text). 1st, past, present questioning	Influence, persuade and argue			Challenging
The Billycart Era	Autobiographical sketch (extract). 1st, past	Entertain			Easily accessible
Letter from Randolph Caldecott	Letter (whole text). 1st, past	Communicate, entertain and describe	✓		Moderately challenging
Letter from Jane Austen	Letter (extract). 1st, past	Communicate, entertain and describe	✓		Challenging
Section 4 Historic events: sharing the impact in a writer's account					
On the sinking of the *Titanic*	Eyewitness account (whole text), 1st, past	Describe and inform	✓		Easily accessible
On the sinking of the *Titanic*	Newspaper report (whole text). 3rd, past	Inform	✓		Easily accessible
The wreck of the *Titanic*	Autobiography (extract). 1st, past	Inform, entertain and explain			Easily accessible
Letter from Major Stubbs	Letter (whole text). 1st, past & present	Communicate and explain			Easily accessible
Goodbye to All That	Autobiography (extract). 1st, past	Record, reflect and influence			Moderately challenging

	Text type	Purpose	Pre-1914	Other cultures	Level of challenge
The Girl in the Red Coat	Autobiography (extract). 1st, present	Record, reflect and influence		✓	Easily accessible
Words to Outlive Us	Historical record (whole text). 1st, past	Document, reflect and influence		✓	Challenging
Section 5 Fact and fiction: exploring why a writer chooses to blur 'truth'					
My Side	Celebrity autobiography (extract). 1st, past	Entertain and inform			Easily accessible
How Do You Want Me?	Celebrity autobiography (extract). 1st, past	Entertain and reflect			Moderately challenging
Billy	Celebrity biography (extract). 3rd, past	Entertain, reflect and analyse			Challenging
Buster's Diaries	Diary (extract). 1st, past & present	Entertain			Easily accessible
The Number Devil	Explanation (extract). 3rd, present	Explain and inform			Easily accessible
A Short History of Nearly Everything	Popular science writing (extract), 3rd, past	Explain and inform			Moderately accessible
Portrait of a Killer	True life crime (extract), 3rd, past	Entertain and persuade			Moderately accessible

This grid will enable teachers to plan routes through the texts other than the ones already suggested by the thematic organisation and activities. So, for example, it would be possible to use this to select a range of varied biographical writing or look at the different ways a writer might present an historical account.

	Intended audience			Teaching points							
	Public audience	Private audience	For children	Create humour	Create tension	Describe people	Describe place	Evoke sympathy/ horror	Relate history	Express point of view	Narrative structure
Spaghetti Bolognese	✓			✓		✓					✓
Cider With Rosie	✓			✓		✓					
Bad Blood	✓			✓		✓					
My Place – Wolverhampton	✓		✓				✓			✓	
Remembering Aunt Marie	✓		✓				✓				✓
The Tiger Ladies	✓					✓			✓		
Wild Swans	✓					✓		✓	✓	✓	
A Middle Eastern Affair	✓						✓				
In Black and White	✓				✓				✓	✓	✓
The Cruellest Miles	✓				✓	✓	✓	✓	✓		✓
Amy Johnson, Queen of the Air	✓				✓				✓		✓

	Intended audience			Teaching points							
	Public audience	Private audience	For children	Create humour	Create tension	Describe people	Describe place	Evoke sympathy/ horror	Relate history	Express point of view	Narrative structure
Terra Incognita	✓				✓	✓	✓	✓	✓		✓
A Covered Wagon Girl		✓	✓				✓		✓		
Don't Let's Go to the Dogs Tonight	✓					✓	✓				✓
Christmas at school	✓					✓	✓				
My East End	✓					✓	✓		✓		
The Billycart Era	✓			✓	✓	✓					✓
Profiting from Child's Play	✓									✓	
Letter from Randolph Caldecott		✓		✓		✓	✓				
Letter from Jane Austen		✓		✓		✓	✓				
Eyewitness – sinking of *Titanic*	✓				✓			✓	✓		✓
Newspaper – sinking of *Titanic*	✓				✓			✓	✓		✓
The wreck of the *Titanic*	✓				✓				✓		

	Intended audience				Teaching points						
	Public audience	Private audience	For children	Create humour	Create tension	Describe people	Describe place	Evoke sympathy/ horror	Relate history	Express point of view	Narrative structure
Letter from Major Stubbs		✓	✓	✓					✓		
Goodbye to All That	✓							✓	✓		
The Girl in the Red Coat	✓				✓	✓		✓	✓		
Words to Outlive Us	✓						✓	✓	✓		
My Side	✓					✓					
How Do You Want Me?	✓			✓		✓		✓			
Billy	✓					✓		✓			
Buster's Diaries	✓			✓							
The Number Devil	✓		✓	✓							✓
A Short History of Nearly Everything	✓								✓		
Portrait of a Killer	✓					✓	✓			✓	✓

Coverage of strategy objectives for Key Stage 3

Section	Extract	Framework objectives		
		Year 7	Year 8	Year 9
1	*Spaghetti Bolognese*	Activity 1: R7, R8 Activity 2: R8	Activity 1: W11, R7, R10 Activity 2: W11, R7	Activity 1: W7 Activity 2: W7
1	*Cider with Rosie*	Activity 1: R8, R9, R12, R14 Activity 2: R8, R9, R12, R14, W19 Activity 3: Wr14	Activity 1: R5, R7, S2 Activity 2: S2, R5, R7, Wr17 Activity 3: Wr7	Activity 1: W7 Activity 2: W7, Wr17 Activity 3: Wr6
1	*Bad Blood*	Activity 1: R8 Activity 2: Wr6, Wr9	Activity 1: W11, R7 Activity 2: Wr6	Activity 1: W7, R11 Activity 2: Wr6, Wr7
1	*My Place – Wolverhampton*	Activity 1: W14, R10, R13 Activity 2: R12 Activity 3: R12 Activity 4e: S8, R15 Activity 5: Wr1, Wr9, S&L13	Activity 1: W12 Activity 2: R5 Activity 3: R5, R7 Activity 4: S7, R10 Activity 5: Wr1, S&L10	Activity 1: S11 Activity 3: W7, R11 Activity 4: S6 Activity 5: R12, Wr1, Wr13, S&L10
1	*Remembering Aunt Marie*	Activity 1: R8 Activity 2: R8, R12, R14 Activity 3: S&L16, S&L17	Activity 1: R5, R10 Activity 2: R7, R7 Activity 3: S&L15	Activity 1: R11 Activity 2: W7, R11 Activity 3: S&L14
1	*The Tiger Ladies*	Activity 1: R8, R12 Activity 2: R12 Activity 3: R8 Activity 5: Wr14	Activity 1: R5 Activity 2: R5 Activity 4: S4	Activity 1: R6 Activity 2: W7 Activity 5: Wr7

Key: **W** = Word level, **S** = Sentence level, **R** = Reading level, **Wr** = Writing level, **S&L** = Speaking and Listening

Section	Extract	Framework objectives		
		Year 7	Year 8	Year 9
1	*Wild Swans*	Activity 1: S8, R8 Activity 2: W14, R14 Activity 3: W14, R14, Wr19	Activity 1: S6, R5, R10 Activity 2: R10 Activity 3: R5, R10, Wr17	Activity 1: R6 Activity 2: W7, R6 Activity 3: R6, Wr17
1	*A Middle Eastern Affair*	Activity 1: R6, S&L12 Activity 2: R12, R13 Activity 3: R12 Activity 4: R12 Activity 5: Wr8, Wr14	Activity 1: S&L12 Activity 2: S2 Activity 4: S2 Activity 5: Wr6	Activity 1: S&L10 Activity 5: Wr6, Wr11
1	Comparing the extracts	Activity 1: R6 Activity 2: R6, Wr6, Wr14 Activity 3: Wr6, Wr9 Activity 4: R2, Wr15, Wr16 Activity 5: R6	Activity 1: Wr5, Wr6 Activity 2: R10, Wr5 Activity 4: R1, Wr13 Activity 5: R11	Activity 2: Wr6, Wr7, Wr11 Activity 3: Wr6, Wr7 Activity 4: Wr13
2	*In Black and White*	Activity 1: R8, R12 Activity 2: R8, R12, Wr19 Activity 3: Wr14	Activity 1: R5 Activity 2: R5, Wr17 Activity 3: Wr7	Activity 1: R6 Activity 2: R6, Wr17 Activity 3: Wr11
2	*The Cruellest Miles*	Activity 1: R2, R6 Activity 2: R8 Activity 3: R8 Activity 4: S11, R12 Activity 5: Wr6, Wr9	Activity 1: R5 Activity 2: R5 Activity 3: R5 Activity 4: R7 Activity 5: Wr5	Activity 3: W7 Activity 4: S6 Activity 5: Wr1, Wr7, Wr17

Key: **W** = Word level, **S** = Sentence level, **R** = Reading level, **Wr** = Writing level, **S&L** = Speaking and Listening

Section	Extract	Framework objectives		
		Year 7F	Year 8	Year 9
2	*Amy Johnson, Queen of the Air*	Activity 1: R6 Activity 2: R7, R8, R13 Activity 3: W14, R12 Activity 4: R12 Activity 5: R12, Wr19	Activity 1: R8 Activity 2: R8 Activity 3: W11 Activity 5: W11, R10, Wr17	Activity 5: Wr17
2	*Terra Incognita, Travels in Antarctica*	Activity 1: R12, R14 Activity 2: R12 Activity 3: R6 Activity 4: R8, R12 Activity 5: S8 Activity 6: R8, R12	Activity 1: R5 Activity 2: W11, R7 Activity 4: R5 Activity 5: S6 Activity 6: R5	Activity 1: W7 Activity 2: W7 Activity 4: W7 Activity 5: S6 Activity 6: W7, Wr17
2	*A Covered Wagon Girl*	Activity 1: R8, R14 Activity 2: S15 Activity 3: R8 Activity 4: Wr10, Wr11, Wr14	Activity 2: S12 Activity 4: Wr12	Activity 4: Wr11
2	*Don't Let's Go to the Dogs Tonight*	Activity 1: R6 Activity 2: R8, R12 Activity 3: R6, R8, R12, Wr19 Activity 4: S7, Wr6, Wr9	Activity 1: R5 Activity 2: R5 Activity 3: R5, Wr17 Activity 4: Wr12	Activity 2: W7 Activity 3: Wr17 Activity 4: Wr7, Wr11
2	Comparing the extracts	Activity 1: R6, Wr1, Wr2, S&L13 Activity 2: R8, R12 Activity 3: Wr14 Activity 4: Wr10, Wr11	Activity 1: Wr1, Wr10, S&L10 Activity 2: R5, R10 Activity 3: Wr5 Activity 4: Wr10, Wr12	Activity 1: S&L10 Activity 2: R7 Activity 3: Wr6, Wr7, Wr11 Activity 4: Wr11

Key: **W** = Word level, **S** = Sentence level, **R** = Reading level, **Wr** = Writing level, **S&L** = Speaking and Listening

Section	Extract	Framework objectives		
		Year 7F	Year 8	Year 9
3	*Christmas at school*	Activity 1: R7, R12 Activity 2: R6 Activity 3: Wr11, Wr14	Activity 2: R16 Activity 3: Wr6	Activity 3: Wr11
3	*My East End*	Activity 1: R8 Activity 2: R2, R6 Activity 3: R7, Wr13 Activity 5: S16 Activity 6: S15, Wr11, S&L1	Activity 5: S12 Activity 6: Wr10	Activity 6: Wr9, S4, S6, S9, S&L3
3	*Profiting from Child's Play*	Activity 1: R2 Activity 2: R7, Wr16 Activity 3: R13 Activity 4: S&L1, S&L13 Activity 5: Wr15, Wr16	Activity 2: R6 Activity 4: R6, S&L10 Activity 5: Wr13	Activity 3: R6 Activity 4: R2, R11 Activity 5: Wr2, Wr14
3	*The Billycart Era*	Activity 1: R14 Activity 2: R8 Activity 3: R7 Activity 4: R15 Activity 5: R12 Activity 6: Wr5, Wr6	Activity 2: R3 Activity 3: R10 Activity 5: R7 Activity 6: Wr7	Activity 6: Wr6, Wr7, S2
3	*Letter from Randolph Caldecott, March 1873*	Activity 1: R2, R4, R7 Activity 2: R12 Activity 3: R8 Activity 4: Wr8, Wr11, Wr14	Activity 2: S12, S13, R7 Activity 3: S13 Activity 4: Wr6, Wr7	Activity 2: R12 Activity 3: S4, W7 Activity 4: Wr6, Wr7, Wr11

Key: **W** = Word level, **S** = Sentence level, **R** = Reading level, **Wr** = Writing level, **S&L** = Speaking and Listening

Section	Extract	Framework objectives		
		Year 7	Year 8	Year 9
3	*Letter from Jane Austen to her sister*	Activity 1: R2, R8 Activity 3: S&L12 Activity 4: Wr6	Activity 1: S13 Activity 2: R7 Activity 3: R7 Activity 4: Wr7	Activity 2: R11 Activity 3: R15 Activity 4: Wr7
3	*Comparing the extracts*	Activity 1: R14 Activity 3: S&L1, S&L12 Activity 5: R14	Activity 1: R10, R11 Activity 3: Wr11, Wr2 Activity 4: S10 Activity 5: W11	Activity 1: R7, R11 Activity 2: R7, R12 Activity 4: Wr9, S3, S9 Activity 5: R11
4	*Charlotte Collyer on the sinking of the Titanic*	Activity 1: R2, R8, R14 Activity 2: R8 Activity 3: R13 Activity 4: Wr14	Activity 1: R5 Activity 3: R11 Activity 4: W1, W6	Activity 4: Wr6, Wr7
4	*Newspaper report on the sinking of the Titanic*	Activity 1: R12, R13 Activity 2: R7 Activity 3: R12, R13 Activity 4: R10, R12, R14, R15, Wr19	Activity 1: R5, R10 Activity 3: R11 Activity 4: R5, R10	
4	*The wreck of the Titanic*	Activity 1: R2, R7 Activity 2: R8 Activity 3: W12, S&L13 Activity 4: Wr1, Wr10	Activity 3: S&L10, R5 Activity 4: S9, Wr2, Wr12	Activity 4: Wr9

Key: W = Word level, **S** = Sentence level, **R** = Reading level, **Wr** = Writing level, **S&L** = Speaking and Listening

Section	Extract	Framework objectives		
		Year 7	Year 8	Year 9
4	*Letter from Major Stubbs to his daughter*	Activity 1: R8 Activity 2: R2, R4, R14 Activity 3: R8, R14 Activity 5: Wr19	Activity 3: W11, R5 Activity 4: R6 Activity 5: Wr7, Wr13	Activity 4: R6 Activity 5: R11
4	*Goodbye to All That*	Activity 1: R8, S&L1, S&L13 Activity 2: R8, R5 Activity 4: R8 Activity 5: R8, R12	Activity 1: R7, S&L10 Activity 5: R6, R7	Activity 5: R11, R15
4	*The Girl in the Red Coat*	Activity 2: R2, R8 Activity 3: R14 Activity 4: R8 Activity 6: S3, S11, Wr7	Activity 1: R5 Activity 2: R5 Activity 3: W11	Activity 1: R6, R11
4	*Words to Outlive Us*	Activity 1: R8, R14 Activity 3: R6	Activity 1: W11, R7 Activity 2: R5, R16 Activity 4: R16	Activity 1: W7 Activity 3: W7 Activity 4: R6
4	*Comparing the extracts*	Activity 1: R6 Activity 2: S&L1, S&L5,	Activity 1: R8, Wr7 Activity 2: R5, S&L10	Activity 1: R7, R11 Activity 2: R6, R7, W7 Activity 3: R6, R7, R9, Wr16, Wr17
5	*My Side*	Activity 1: R8 Activity 2: S&L12, S&L13 Activity 3: R2, R4, R7 Activity 4: S&L12	Activity 2: S&L10, Wr10 Activity 3: R5 Activity 4: R6, S&L10	Activity 3: Wr17, S&L2 Activity 4: S&L9 Activity 5: Wr7

Key: **W** = Word level, **S** = Sentence level, **R** = Reading level, **Wr** = Writing level, **S&L** = Speaking and Listening

Section	Extract	Framework objectives		
		Year 7	Year 8	Year 9
5	*How Do You Want Me?*	Activity 1: R8, R13, R14 Activity 4: R14, R7, Activity 6: R6, R8	Activity 2: R7 Activity 4: R7 Activity 6: R5 Activity 7: R6 Activity 8: R6	Activity 7: R11, Wr16 Activity 8: Wr17
5	*Billy*	Activity 1: R8 Activity 2: R8 Activity 3: R12, R14 Activity 6: S&L1, S&L12	Activity 2: R6 Activity 4: R7 Activity 6: R5	Activity 5: R11 Activity 6: R5
5	*Buster's Diaries*	Activity 1: R8, R12 Activity 2: Wr6, Wr9	Activity 1: W13, S12, R8 Activity 2: Wr7, Wr8	Activity 1: W7, R11 Activity 2: Wr5, Wr7
5	*The Number Devil*	Activity 1: R7, R12, R15 Activity 2: R7, R12, R15, Wr19	Activity 1: R10, R11 Activity 2: R10, R11, Wr17	Activity 2: Wr17
	A Short History of Nearly Everything	Activity 1: W14, R8, R12, R13, R14 Activity 2: Wr11	Activity 1: R11, W12, Wr17 Activity 2: Wr11	Activity 1: S4 Activity 2: Wr12
5	*Portrait of a Killer*	Activity 1: R8, R9, R12 Activity 2: Wr9, Wr14	Activity 1: R5, R6, R7 Activity 2: Wr6	Activity 1: R11 Activity 2: Wr7, Wr11
5	*Comparing the extracts*	Activity 1: Wr9 Activity 2: R6	Activity 1: Wr8 Activity 2: R4	Activity 1: Wr7 Activity 2: R7

Key: **W** = Word level, **S** = Sentence level, **R** = Reading level, **Wr** = Writing level, **S&L** = Speaking and Listening

The best in classic and

Jane Austen

Elizabeth Laird

Beverley Naidoo Roddy Doyle

Robert Swindells

George Orwell

Charles Dickens

Charlotte Brontë

Jan Mark

Anne Fine

Anthony Horowitz